The Albemarle Library for Schools

*

THE ALBEMARLE BOOK
OF MODERN VERSE
2

The Albemarle Book of
MODERN VERSE

2

Edited by F. E. S. Finn, B.A.

Head of English Department
Exmouth School

*

WITH AN INTRODUCTION BY
Howard Sergeant

JOHN MURRAY

FIFTY ALBEMARLE STREET LONDON

First published 1961
Reprinted 1964, 1965, 1966, 1969

Printed in Great Britain by Jarrold and Sons Ltd, Norwich

7195 0442 2

PREFACE

This anthology is compiled from verse written or published during the last thirty-five years. It is not a book of 'children's verse'; it is a selection of modern verse chosen for pupils aged fourteen to nineteen years. Volume 1 is intended for the middle and Volume 2 for the upper school.

The needs and capabilities of such readers—so far as one school-master is able to gauge them—have been the editor's guiding principle. Hence, there has been no attempt to include poets who 'ought' to be represented. Many, such as Edith Sitwell and Ezra Pound, are un-represented for a variety of reasons—content, style and difficulty, or occasionally because the poems of theirs which are suitable have already been frequently anthologized. Little narrative verse has been included, not only from reasons of space, but also on the ground that pupils of this age-group should be interested in the ideas, feelings and experiences which are characteristic of lyrical verse. Again, no attempt has been made to show every aspect or phase of a poet's work; this is better left to anthologies containing the work of a smaller number of poets. In cases where poets have been productive over a long period (for example, Walter de la Mare, or Wilfrid Gibson), late rather than early or well-known poems have been chosen. While poems which are very familiar have generally been avoided, some have been included for special reasons: for instance T. S. Eliot's 'Journey of the Magi' because of the opportunities it gives for comparison with W. R. Rodgers's 'The Journey of the Magi', and other poems. Much of the work is by writers living in this country, but there is a substantial contribution from Commonwealth and American poets.

The arrangement is according to authors; but the books have been compiled to provide ample opportunity for comparison of poems with similar subjects and styles. It is hoped that these two volumes, providing an unusually wide selection of recent verse, will meet the need in secondary schools for a 'modern' anthology which can be appreciated by young readers who already have some acquaintance with the older poets.

F.E.S.F.

INTRODUCTION

Whatever contemporary poetry may owe to traditional practice, there can be little doubt that for many of us poetry of today seems far more complex than that of any earlier period. To a certain extent difficulty arises because, being confronted by something new, we are compelled to make a genuine effort to think for ourselves, whereas the poetry written in other ages has already been assimilated for us; we have been taught what to expect and, in some cases, what we ought to admire. This is as it should be; for a good poem presents us with a fresh experience, or a re-ordering of past experience, and should assist us to obtain a clearer perspective of the world in general, and of human behaviour as it is, not merely as we should like it to be.

Nevertheless, it would be fair to say that much of our difficulty is due to changes which have taken place during the last fifty years or so. The poet is particularly sensitive to current ideas, to the problems, tensions, preoccupations, moral attitudes and general way of life of the age and society to which he belongs; and the present age is one in which new knowledge and ideas have utterly changed man's conception, not only of the universe, but of the world within himself. Our acquaintance with the writings of such poets as Shakespeare, Blake and Wordsworth, has made it clear to us that the poet, owing to the peculiar nature of his insight, may be aware of powerful hidden forces at work in the mind long before the scientific terms to define them and their functions have been invented. It is recorded that when Freud was greeted by an enthusiastic admirer as 'the discoverer of the unconscious', he pointedly remarked—'The poets and the philosophers before me discovered the unconscious. What I discovered was the scientific method by which the unconscious can be studied.' So that, although psychology is properly concerned with what has always been the raw material of the poet, as a result of Freud's systematic explorations of the human mind, the poet has become more conscious of himself and of the actual processes involved in the transformation of his experience into poetry. For instance, though it may not at first be apparent, when Robert Graves writes:

> Of spirits in the web-hung room
> Up above the stable,
> Groans, knockings in the gloom,
> The dancing table,

Of demons in the dry well
That cheep and mutter,
Clanging of an unseen bell,
Blood choking the gutter . . .

in his poem entitled 'The Haunted House' (see p. 66) he is referring, not to some ghost-ridden mansion, but to his own mind.

If man's conception of himself and of his own mental processes has been radically altered during the last fifty years, his conception of the external universe has undergone a change no less revolutionary. So much so that it has been necessary for some purposes to discard Newtonian ideas of time, space, gravity and matter, and to replace what had long been accepted as fundamental laws of nature by working principles more applicable to the facts newly discovered by observation and experiment, even if outside the normal range of everyday experience. Meanwhile, the astronomers have found the stellar universe to be immeasurably vaster than has ever been conceived before, and our own system to be but one of the countless galaxies of stars, to say nothing of the spiral nebulae by which the earth is surrounded as far as the radio-telescopic eye can probe. To give any adequate account of the new creative potencies which, together with the traditions and techniques of the past, have exerted their influence upon contemporary poetry it would, therefore, be necessary to consider the scientific ideas which have helped to change the pattern of our thought and belief, and this is hardly the place for such an exegesis. I hope that, at least, I have been able to point to a vital relationship between poetry and life as we know it today.

It would be foolish to claim that modern poets succeed in keeping themselves so well informed on the latest scientific theories that they can assimilate them and transform them into poetry, but it would be equally foolish to maintain that they can remain unaffected by these new conceptions of man and the universe and yet have anything valid to say to us. One might insist that poets, being susceptible to changes in thought concerned with man in relation to his environment, can hardly help themselves. They must be of their own age and attempt to come to terms with the material around them. In one way or another most of the poets in this collection tend to reflect in their work the uncertainty of the period and their sense of insecurity—and in this respect they give expression to our own feelings, for we are all becoming more and more aware of the complexity of the world in which we live, whilst growing less confident in man's ability to utilize his scientific and technical resources for the benefit of the human race. If, fundamentally, the subjects of poetry remain the same as always, they have to be set against a completely different background—a background, let it be said, that is assuming ever more complicated proportions. Some of the poems in this anthology are so relevant to the present age that they could hardly have been written at any other time in history (*i.e.* Auden's 'Refugee Blues'; Gascoyne's 'Spring MCMXL'; Holloway's 'The Quick and the Dead'; and Jeffers's 'The Purse-Seine', amongst others).

Yet, whether the poet belongs to a comparatively static period, or to a period in which new discoveries and knowledge are rapidly changing man's outlook, the problem is always the basic one of language. It may be expedient for scientists to invent a mathematical language incomprehensible to the layman in order to convey their theories with greater precision, but the poet must grapple with the complexities of his age through the medium of words which have already accumulated a weight of meaning from centuries of human experience. To some extent, therefore, he cannot escape from tradition, even if it were desirable. Yet, on the other hand, he must endeavour to exploit all the resources of language by whatever means lie in his power, so that his poetry will properly express his own response to life. If he is successful he may add new associations and values to the words he uses. In this way tradition is continually being extended.

One of the advantages of possessing as comprehensive an anthology as Mr Finn's, then, is that we are able to compare the language, techniques and ideas of poets throughout the English-speaking world, for assembled here are poems written during the last twenty or thirty years by some of the most outstanding American, Australian, British, Canadian, New Zealand and South African poets. There are, of course, several modern anthologies already in use in our schools, but I have yet to see a collection in a schools' edition which covers anything like so much ground as this volume, or which affords such an abundance of first-rate poetry suitable for introduction to young students. Since we all have our favourite poets, it will be possible to quarrel with some of the omissions, or to dispute the claims of some of the poems included, but that would be to miss the point. For though it is hoped that this selection of poems will give real and lasting enjoyment, it has been designed primarily for the use of schools and it is not intended to be representative of all the best poets writing today. If, as a result of this volume, students discover for themselves that modern poetry is neither so difficult nor so obscure as they have been led to believe, it will be due in large measure to the conscientious and skilful manner in which Mr Finn has performed his editorial task.

It is indeed pleasing to be able to recommend as eminently suitable for school use an anthology which not only presents a wide range of contemporary poetry, but which, whilst accepting the challenge of our time, so admirably demonstrates the continuing vitality of the English poetic tradition.

HOWARD SERGEANT

CONTENTS

'ALL LOVELY THINGS'

All lovely things will have an ending,   *Conrad*
  All lovely things will fade and die,   *Aiken*
And youth, that's now so bravely spending,
  Will beg a penny by and by.

Fine ladies all are soon forgotten,
  And goldenrod is dust when dead,
The sweetest flesh and flowers are rotten
  And cobwebs tent the brightest head.

Come back, true love! Sweet youth, return!—
  But time goes on, and will, unheeding,
Though hands will reach, and eyes will yearn,
  And the wild days set true hearts bleeding.

Come back, true love! Sweet youth, remain!—
  But goldenrod and daisies wither,
And over them blows autumn rain,
  They pass, they pass, and know not whither.

BRIGHTON

  All-electric, down from London   *John*
  Every hour the green trains run,   *Arlott*
  Bearing tribes of worshippers
  To the doubtful Brighton sun,

  Postcards of the Sussex Downs,
  Ice-rinks, music-halls and beer,
  Dance-halls, snack-bars and the rain
  On the domed and garnished pier.

  There's an elegant Adam fireplace
  In a third-rate dancing-club,
  A blackened print of Prinny
  In a seedy, smoke-fumed pub,

  Regency houses, row on row,
  In crescent, square and street,
  With pediment, pillar and portico,
  'BED AND BREAKFAST' all complete.

Strange-wrought Gothic street-lamps,
Churches a-gleam with tile
Jostle the chrome and marble
Of super-cinema style.

From the tomb-like cold Pavilion,
Drawing-Rooms and Dome,
Regency ghosts come sweeping
Through the town that was their home.

Do they see the plaster peeling?
The fly-blows on the ceiling?
Regency houses tumbled down?
Hove another, *nicer* town?
The Phaeton gone for the family car?
Electric light in the Oyster Bar?
And buses bluing the salt sea air
Under the trees in Castle Square?

And would they return to Hell by way
Of Brighton beach on a summer day?
Trip with trippers up-to-date?
And, Regency ghosts immaculate,
Bucks and doxies, pair by pair,
Past the whelk-stalls and through the profanity
Struggle down the steep stone stair
Into this huddle of hot humanity?

TEA WITH MY AUNTS

Tea with my aunts at half past four—
Tea in a world without a war;
The Widow-Queen is still alive
In grandpa's house in Albert Drive,
And firm the monkey-puzzle tree
He planted at the Jubilee.

A frilly, fragile cup of tea
Unsafely balanced on my knee,
Aunt Anna mellows as I take
Another slice of home-made cake;
She rustles in her stiff grey gown
And takes her endless knitting down.

2

A chastely-ringed and blue-veined hand,
A weak, white neck in velvet band,
With modest touch Aunt Susan plays
The tranquil 'Sheep May Safely Graze'
Of Bach, the tune she used to play,
On Sunday evenings years away,
To whiskered men of gentle sort
Who paid her strained and stately court.

The Landseer cattle on the wall,
The massy antlers in the hall,
The monumental two-year clock,
A faith in class as firm as rock,
And all the house are just the same
As on the day the family came,
Firm barred against the new and strange
And devil-prompted thoughts of change.

Those gilt-edged shares will never drop,
But yearly yield a steady crop
To feed a world of certain grace,
Where servants know their proper place.
The bombs that broke the windows here
Have not disturbed the atmosphere.

A LITTLE GUIDE TO WINCHESTER

At Winchester the smell of guide-books lies
Across the streets with mediæval names,
And snap-views of the long Cathedral rise
Through alley-ways and leaded window-frames.

Along the High Street, fussing traffic pours
Until the Butter Cross juts out: then stops—
By old St Maurice's half-hidden doors,
And shoes and shirts in mild unbrazen shops.

See, cycling blithely through the grumbling cars,
A Wykehamist, with brightly banded tie;
There, in the basket on his handlebars,
The biscuits, cakes and books he came to buy.

Now, like a matron, over-jewelled and laced,
The Gothic Guildhall, by Sir Gilbert Scott,
And phoney-Tudor, beam-and-plaster faced,
The jeweller's shop Hostel of God-Begot.

Silk stockings and fur coats and dove-grey gowns
Take tea and muffins in a Norman keep;
While, as the sun moves round behind the downs,
The Close-housed clergy court cathedral sleep
In rooms so old a man is but a guest
Who lives a lifetime there. Dog-collars loosed
They take their sermon-bearing tithe of rest
In houses that are stone-spelt peace on earth.

In other—harsh-lined—parlours, stiffly sit
Those unloved spinsters and unloving wives,
Who chatter acid as they flickly knit,
And detail spite of other people's lives.

Before the broad-set, idling water-mill,
Down where the green-flanked buses turn and wait,
King Alfred wears the crown of Wessex still.
He lifts his broadsword to the western gate
And, in obedience to his statued will,
The little Saxons muster to defend
Their stricken, narrow houses on the hill,
The Hardy-Trollope-Walpole city's end.

'O WHAT IS THAT SOUND?'

W. H. Auden

O what is that sound which so thrills the ear
   Down in the valley drumming, drumming?
Only the scarlet soldiers, dear,
   The soldiers coming.

O what is that light I see flashing so clear
   Over the distance brightly, brightly?
Only the sun on their weapons, dear,
   As they step lightly.

O what are they doing with all that gear,
   What are they doing this morning, this morning?
Only their usual manœuvres, dear,
   Or perhaps a warning.

O why have they left the road down there,
    Why are they suddenly wheeling, wheeling?
Perhaps a change in their orders, dear.
    Why are you kneeling?

O haven't they stopped for the doctor's care,
    Haven't they reined their horses, their horses?
Why, they are none of them wounded, dear,
    None of these forces.

O is it the parson they want, with white hair,
    Is it the parson, is it, is it?
No, they are passing his gateway, dear,
    Without a visit.

O it must be the farmer who lives so near.
    It must be the farmer so cunning, so cunning?
They have passed the farmyard already, dear,
    And now they are running.

O where are you going? Stay with me here!
    Were the vows you swore deceiving, deceiving?
No, I promised to love you, dear,
    But I must be leaving.

O it's broken the lock and splintered the door,
    O it's the gate where they're turning, turning;
Their boots are heavy on the floor
    And their eyes are burning.

REFUGEE BLUES

Say this city has ten million souls,
Some are living in mansions, some are living in holes:
Yet there's no place for us, my dear, yet there's no place for us.

Once we had a country and we thought it fair,
Look in the atlas and you'll find it there:
We cannot go there now, my dear, we cannot go there now.

In the village churchyard there grows an old yew,
Every spring it blossoms anew;
Old passports can't do that, my dear, old passports can't do that.

W. H. Auden   The consul banged the table and said;
'If you've no passport, you're officially dead':
But we are still alive, my dear, but we are still alive.

Went to a committee; they offered me a chair;
Asked me politely to return next year:
But where shall we go today, my dear, but where shall we go today?

Came to a public meeting; the speaker got up and said:
'If we let them in, they will steal our daily bread';
He was talking of you and me, my dear, he was talking of you and me.

Thought I heard the thunder rumbling in the sky,
It was Hitler over Europe, saying: 'They must die';
O we were in his mind, my dear, O we were in his mind.

Saw a poodle in a jacket fastened with a pin,
Saw a door open and a cat let in:
But they weren't German Jews, my dear, but they weren't German
    Jews.

Went down the harbour and stood upon the quay,
Saw the fish swimming as if they were free:
Only ten feet away, my dear, only ten feet away.

Walked through a wood, saw the birds in the trees;
They had no politicians and sang at their ease:
They weren't the human race, my dear, they weren't the human race.

Dreamt I saw a building with a thousand floors,
A thousand windows and a thousand doors;
Not one of them was ours, my dear, not one of them was ours.

Stood on a great plain in the falling snow;
Ten thousand soldiers marched to and fro:
Looking for you and me, my dear, looking for you and me.

MUSÉE DES BEAUX ARTS

About suffering they were never wrong,
The Old Masters: how well they understood
Its human position; how it takes place
While someone else is eating or opening a window or just
    walking dully along;

6

How, when the aged are reverently, passionately waiting
For the miraculous birth, there always must be
Children who did not specially want it to happen, skating
On a pond at the edge of the wood:
They never forgot
That even the dreadful martyrdom must run its course
Anyhow in a corner, some untidy spot
Where the dogs go on with their doggy life and the torturer's horse
Scratches its innocent behind on a tree.

In Breughel's *Icarus*, for instance: how everything turns away
Quite leisurely from the disaster; the ploughman may
Have heard the splash, the forsaken cry,
But for him it was not an important failure; the sun shone
As it had to on the white legs disappearing into the green
Water; and the expensive delicate ship that must have seen
Something amazing, a boy falling out of the sky,
Had somewhere to get to and sailed calmly on.

'AS I WALKED OUT ONE EVENING'

As I walked out one evening,
  Walking down Bristol Street,
The crowds upon the pavement
  Were fields of harvest wheat.

And down by the brimming river
  I heard a lover sing
Under an arch of the railway:
  'Love has no ending.

'I'll love you, dear, I'll love you
  Till China and Africa meet
And the river jumps over the mountain
  And the salmon sing in the street.

'I'll love you till the ocean
  Is folded and hung up to dry
And the seven stars go squawking
  Like geese about the sky.

'The years shall run like rabbits
  For in my arms I hold
The Flower of the Ages
  And the first love of the world.'

But all the clocks in the city
   Began to whirr and chime:
'O let not Time deceive you,
   You cannot conquer Time.

'In the burrows of the Nightmare
   Where Justice naked is,
Time watches from the shadow
   And coughs when you would kiss.

'In headaches and in worry
   Vaguely life leaks away,
And Time will have his fancy
   Tomorrow or today.

'Into many a green valley
   Drifts the appalling snow;
Time breaks the threaded dances
   And the diver's brilliant bow.

'O plunge your hands in water,
   Plunge them in up to the wrist;
Stare, stare in the basin
   And wonder what you've missed.

'The glacier knocks in the cupboard,
   The desert sighs in the bed,
And the crack in the tea/cup opens
   A lane to the land of the dead.

'Where the beggars raffle the banknotes
   And the Giant is enchanting to Jack,
And the Lily/white Boy is a Roarer
   And Jill goes down on her back.

'O look, look in the mirror,
   O look in your distress;
Life remains a blessing
   Although you cannot bless.

'O stand, stand at the window
   As the tears scald and start;
You shall love your crooked neighbour
   With your crooked heart.'

It was late, late in the evening,
The lovers they were gone;
The clocks had ceased their chiming
And the deep river ran on.

WILD BEES

Often in summer on a tarred bridge plank standing
Or downstream between willows, a safe Ophelia drifting
In a rented boat—I had seen them come and go,
Those wild bees swift as tigers, their gauze wings a-glitter
In passionless industry, clustering black at the crevice
Of a rotten cabbage tree, where their hive was hidden low.

But never strolled too near. Till one half-cloudy evening
Of ripe January, my friends and I
Came, gloved and masked to the eyes like plundering desperadoes
To smoke them out. Quiet beside the stagnant river
We trod wet grasses down, hearing the crickets chitter
And waiting for light to drain from the wounded sky.

Before we reached the hive their sentries saw us
And sprang invisible through the darkening air;
Stabbed, and died in stinging. The hive woke. Poisonous fuming
Of sulphur filled the hollow trunk, and crawling
Blue flame sputtered: yet still their suicidal
Live raiders dived and clung to our hands and hair.

O it was Carthage under the Roman torches
Or loud with flames and falling timber, Troy.
A job well botched: half of the honey melted
And half the rest young grubs. Through earth-black smouldering
   ashes
And maimed bees groaning, we drew out our plunder—
Little enough their gold, and slight our joy.

Fallen then the city of instinctive wisdom.
Tragedy is written distinct and small:
A hive burned on a cool night in summer.
But loss is a precious stone to me, a nectar
Distilled in time, preaching the truth of winter
To the fallen heart that does not cease to fall.

*James K.
Baxter*

ANEMONES FOR MISS AUSTEN

Bernard
Bergonzi

Indeed a sweet and knowing lady,
quietly scribbling away her time;
the geographer of a gentle clime
where only the lanes were shady,
the poor kept decently out of sight,
and the neat old-fashioned carriages
manœuvred the county marriages,
where the curates came off worst, as well they might.

The cool young heroines got their men,
and in due time were suitably wed.
None of the details escaped her pen.

And yet, somehow she never quite said
a word about what happened then,
how they managed with breakfast or bed.

ON A PORTRAIT OF A DEAF MAN

John
Betjeman

The kind old face, the egg-shaped head,
    The tie, discreetly loud,
The loosely fitting shooting clothes,
    A closely fitting shroud.

He liked old City dining-rooms,
    Potatoes in their skin,
But now his mouth is wide to let
    The London clay come in.

He took me on long silent walks
    In country lanes when young,
He knew the name of ev'ry bird
    But not the song it sung.

And when he could not hear me speak
    He smiled and looked so wise
That now I do not like to think
    Of maggots in his eyes.

He liked the rain-washed Cornish air
    And smell of ploughed-up soil,
He liked a landscape big and bare
    And painted it in oil.

10

But least of all he liked that place
  Which hangs on Highgate Hill
Of soaked Carrara-covered earth
  For Londoners to fill.

He would have liked to say good-bye,
  Shake hands with many friends,
In Highgate now his finger-bones
  Stick through his finger-ends.

You, God, who treat him thus and thus,
  Say 'Save his soul and pray.'
You ask me to believe You and
  I only see decay.

DEATH IN LEAMINGTON

She died in the upstairs bedroom
  By the light of the ev'ning star
That shone through the plate glass window
  From over Leamington Spa.

Beside her the lonely crochet
  Lay patiently and unstirred,
But the fingers that would have work'd it
  Were dead as the spoken word.

And Nurse came in with the tea-things
  Breast high 'mid the stands and chairs—
But Nurse was alone with her own little soul
  And the things were alone with theirs.

She bolted the big round window,
  She let the blinds unroll,
She set a match to the mantle,
  She covered the fire with coal.

And 'Tea!' she said in a tiny voice
  'Wake up! It's nearly *five*.'
Oh! Chintzy, chintzy cheeriness,
  Half dead and half alive!

Do you know that the stucco is peeling?
  Do you know that the heart will stop?
From those yellow Italianate arches
  Do you hear the plaster drop?

John
Betjeman

Nurse looked at the silent bedstead,
  At the grey, decaying face,
As the calm of a Leamington ev'ning
  Drifted into the place.

She moved the table of bottles
  Away from the bed to the wall;
And tiptoeing gently over the stairs
  Turned down the gas in the hall.

THE VILLAGE INN

'The village inn, the dear old inn,
So ancient, clean and free from sin,
True centre of our rural life
Where Hodge sits down beside his wife
And talks of Marx and nuclear fission
With all a rustic's intuition.
Ah, more than church or school or hall,
The village inn's the heart of all.'
So spake the brewer's P.R.O.,
A man who really ought to know,
For he is paid for saying so.
And then he kindly gave to me
A lovely coloured booklet free.
'Twas full of prose that sang the praise
Of coaching inns in Georgian days,
Showing how public-houses are
More modern than the motor-car,
More English than the weald or wold
And almost equally as old,
And run for love and not for gold,
Until I felt a filthy swine
For loathing beer and liking wine,
And rotten to the very core
For thinking village inns a bore,
And village bores more sure to roam
To village inns than stay at home.
And then I thought I *must* be wrong,
So up I rose and went along
To that old village alehouse where
In neon lights is written 'Bear'.

Ah, where's the inn that once I knew
    With brick and chalky wall
Up which the knobbly pear-tree grew
    For fear the place would fall?

Oh, that old pot-house isn't there,
    It wasn't worth our while;
You'll find we have rebuilt 'The Bear'
    In Early Georgian style.

But winter jasmine used to cling
    With golden stars a-shine
Where rain and wind would wash and swing
    The crudely painted sign.

And where's the roof of golden thatch?
    The chimney-stack of stone?
The crown-glass panes that used to match
    Each sunset with their own?

Oh now the walls are red and smart,
    The roof has emerald tiles.
The neon sign's a work of art
    And visible for miles.

The bar inside was papered green,
    The settles grained like oak,
The only light was paraffin,
    The woodfire used to smoke.

And photographs from far and wide
    Were hung around the room:
The hunt, the church, the football side,
    And Kitchener of Khartoum.

Our air-conditioned bars are lined
    With washable material,
The stools are steel, the taste refined,
    Hygienic and ethereal.

Hurrah, hurrah, for hearts of oak!
    Away with inhibitions!
For here's a place to sit and soak
    In sanit'ry conditions.

13

CHRISTMAS

John
Betjeman

The bells of waiting Advent ring,
    The Tortoise stove is lit again
And lamp-oil light across the night
    Has caught the streaks of winter rain
In many a stained-glass window sheen
From Crimson Lake to Hooker's Green.

The holly in the windy hedge
    And round the Manor House the yew
Will soon be stripped to deck the ledge,
    The altar, font and arch and pew,
So that the villagers can say
'The church looks nice' on Christmas Day.

Provincial public houses blaze
    And Corporation tramcars clang,
On lighted tenements I gaze
    Where paper decorations hang,
And bunting in the red Town Hall
Says 'Merry Christmas to you all.'

And London shops on Christmas Eve
    Are strung with silver bells and flowers
As hurrying clerks the City leave
    To pigeon-haunted classic towers,
And marbled clouds go scudding by
The many-steepled London sky.

And girls in slacks remember Dad,
    And oafish louts remember Mum,
And sleepless children's hearts are glad,
    And Christmas-morning bells say 'Come!'
Even to shining ones who dwell
Safe in the Dorchester Hotel.

And is it true? And is it true,
    This most tremendous tale of all,
Seen in a stained-glass window's hue,
    A Baby in an ox's stall?
The Maker of the stars and sea
Become a Child on earth for me?

14

And is it true? For if it is,
   No loving fingers tying strings
Around those tissued fripperies,
   The sweet and silly Christmas things,
Bath salts and inexpensive scent
And hideous tie so kindly meant,

No love that in a family dwells,
   No carolling in frosty air,
Nor all the steeple-shaking bells
   Can with this single Truth compare—
That God was Man in Palestine
And lives today in Bread and Wine.

BRISTOL

Green upon the flooded Avon shone the after-storm-wet sky
Quick the struggling withy branches let the leaves of Autumn fly
And a star shone over Bristol, wonderfully far and high.

Ringers in an oil-lit belfry—Bitton? Kelston? who shall say?—
Smoothly practising a plain course, caverned out the dying day
As their melancholy music flooded up and ebbed away.

Then all Somerset was round me and I saw the clippers ride,
High above the moonlit houses, triple-masted on the tide,
By the tall embattled church-towers of the Bristol waterside.

And an undersong to branches dipping into pools and wells
Out of multitudes of elm trees over leagues of hills and dells
Was the mathematic pattern of a plain course on the bells.

SUNDAY MORNING, KING'S CAMBRIDGE

File into yellow candle light, fair choristers of King's
   Lost in the shadowy silence of canopied Renaissance stalls
In blazing glass above the dark glow skies and thrones and wings
   Blue, ruby, gold, and green between the whiteness of the walls
And with what rich precision the stonework soars and springs
   To fountain out a spreading vault—a shower that never falls.

The white of windy Cambridge courts, the cobbles brown and dry,
The gold of plaster Gothic with ivy overgrown,
The apple⁄red, the silver fronts, the wide green flats and high,
The yellowing elm⁄trees circled out on islands of their own—
Oh, here behold all colours change that catch the flying sky
To waves of pearly light that heave along the shafted stone.

In far East Anglian churches, the clasped hands lying long
Recumbent on sepulchral slabs or effigied in brass
Buttress with prayer this vaulted roof so white and light and strong
And countless congregations as the generations pass
Join choir and great crowned organ case, in centuries of song
To praise Eternity contained in Time and coloured glass.

CORNWALL IN CHILDHOOD

from *Summoned by Bells*

Come, Hygiene, goddess of the growing boy,
I here salute thee in Sanatogen!
Anaemic girls need Virol, but for me
Be Scott's Emulsion, rusks, and Mellin's Food,
Cod⁄liver oil and malt, and for my neck
Wright's Coal Tar Soap, Euthymol for my teeth.
Come, friends of Hygiene, Electricity
And those young twins, Free Thought and clean Fresh Air:
Attend the long express from Waterloo
That takes us down to Cornwall. Tea⁄time shows
The small fields waiting, every blackthorn hedge
Straining inland before the south⁄west gale.
The emptying train, wind in the ventilators,
Puffs out of Egloskerry to Tresméer
Through minty meadows, under bearded trees
And hills upon whose sides the clinging farms
Hold Bible Christians. Can it really be
That this same carriage came from Waterloo?
On Wadebridge station what a breath of sea
Scented the Camel valley! Cornish air,
Soft Cornish rains, and silence after steam . . .
As out of Derry's stable came the brake
To drag us up those long, familiar hills,
Past haunted woods and oil⁄lit farms and on
To far Trebetherick by the sounding sea.
Oh what a host of questions in me rose:

Were spring tides here or neap? And who was down?
Had Mr Rosevear built himself a house?
Was there another wreck upon Doom Bar?
The carriage lamps lit up the pennywort
And fennel in the hedges of the lane;
Huge slugs were crawling over slabs of slate;
Then, safe in bed, I watched the long legg'd fly
With red transparent body tap the walls
And fizzle in the candle flame and drag
Its poisonous-looking abdomen away
To somewhere out of sight and out of mind,
While through the open window came the roar
Of full Atlantic rollers on the beach.
    Then before breakfast down toward the sea
I ran alone, monarch of miles of sand,
Its shining stretches satin-smooth and vein'd.
I felt beneath bare feet the lugworm casts
And walked, where only gulls and oyster-catchers
Had stepped before me to the water's edge.
The morning tide flowed in to welcome me,
The fan-shaped scallop shells, the backs of crabs,
The bits of driftwood worn to reptile shapes,
The heaps of bladder-wrack the tide had left,
(Which, lifted up, sent sandhoppers to leap
In hundreds round me) answered 'Welcome back!'
Along the links and under cold Bray Hill
Fresh water pattered from an iris marsh
And drowned the golf-balls on its stealthy way
Over the slates in which the elvers hid,
And spread across the beach. I used to stand,
A speculative water engineer—
Here I would plan a dam and there a sluice
And thus divert the stream, creating lakes,
A chain of locks descending to the sea.
Inland I saw, above the tamarisks,
From various villas morning breakfast smoke
Which warned me then of mine; so up the lane
I wandered home contented, full of plans,
Pulling a length of pink convolvulus
Whose blossoms, almost as I picked them, died.
    Bright as the morning sea those early days!
Though there were tears, and sand thrown in my eyes,
And punishments and smells of mackintosh,
Long barefoot climbs to fetch the morning milk,
Terrors from hissing geese and angry shouts,

Slammed doors and waitings and a sense of dread,
Still warm as shallow sea-pools in the sun
And welcoming to me the girls and boys.
  Wet rocks on which our bathing dresses dried;
Small coves deserted in our later years
For more adventurous inlets down the coast:
Paralysis when climbing up the cliff—
Too steep to reach the top, too far to fall,
Tumbling to death in seething surf below,
A ledge just wide enough to lodge one's foot,
A sea-pink clump the only thing to clutch,
Cold wave-worn slate so mercilessly smooth
And no one near and evening coming on—
Till Ralph arrived: 'Now put your left foot here.
Give us your hand' . . . and back across the years
I swing to safety with old friends again.
Small seem they now, those once tremendous cliffs,
Diminished now those joy-enclosing bays.

  Childhood is measured out by sounds and smells
And sights, before the dark of reason grows.
Ears! Hear again the wild sou'westers whine!
Three days on end would the September gale
Slam at our bungalows; three days on end
Rattling cheap doors and making tempers short.
It mattered not, for then enormous waves
House-high rolled thunderous on Greenaway,
Flinging up spume and shingle to the cliffs.
Unmoved amid the foam, the cormorant
Watched from its peak. In all the roar and swirl
The still and small things gained significance.
Somehow the freckled cowrie would survive
And prawns hang waiting in their watery woods;
Deep in the noise there was a core of peace;
Deep in my heart a warm security.
  Nose! Smell again the early morning smells:
Congealing bacon and my father's pipe;
The after-breakfast freshness out of doors
Where sun had dried the heavy dew and freed
Acres of thyme to scent the links and lawns;
The rotten apples on our shady path
Where blowflies settled upon squashy heaps,
Intent and gorging; at the garden gate
Reek of Solignum on the wooden fence;
Mint round the spring, and fennel in the lane,

And honeysuckle wafted from the hedge;
The Lynams' cess-pool like a body-blow;
Then, clean, medicinal and cold—the sea.
'Breathe in the ozone, John. It's iodine.'
But which is iodine and which is drains?
Salt and hot sun on rubber water-wings . . .
Home to the luncheon smell of Irish stew
And washing-up stench from the kitchen sink
Because the sump is blocked. The afternoons
Brought coconut smell of gorse; at Mably's farm
Sweet scent of drying cowdung; then the moist
Exhaling of the earth in Shilla woods—
First earth encountered after days of sand.
Evening brought back the gummy smell of toys
And fishy stink of glue and Stickphast paste,
And sleep inside the laundriness of sheets.

   Eyes! See again the rock-face in the lane,
Years before tarmac and the motor-car.
Across the estuary Stepper Point
Stands, still unquarried, black against the sun;
On its Atlantic face the cliffs fall sheer.
Look down into the weed world of the lawn—
The devil's-coach-horse beetle hurries through,
Lifting its tail up as I bar the way
To further flowery jungles.
                   See once more
The Padstow ferry, worked by oar and sail,
Her outboard engine always going wrong,
Ascend the slippery quay's up-ended slate,
The sea-weed hanging from the harbour wall.
Hot was the pavement under, as I gazed
At lanterns, brass, rope and ships' compasses
In the marine-store window on the quay.
The shoe-shop in the square was cool and dark.
The Misses Quintrell, fancy stationers,
Had most to show me—dialect tales in verse
Published in Truro (Netherton and Worth)
And model lighthouses of serpentine.
Climb the steep hill to where that belt of elm
Circles the town and church tower, reached by lanes
Whose ferny ramparts shelter toadflax flowers
And periwinkles. See hydrangeas bloom
In warm back-gardens full of fuchsia bells.
To the returning ferry soon draws near
Our own low bank of sand-dunes; then the walk

Over a mile of quicksand evening-cold.
It all is there, excitement for the eyes,
Imagined ghosts on unfrequented roads
Gated and winding up through broom and gorse
Out of the parish, on to who knows where?
What pleasure, as the oil-lamp sparkled gold
On cut-glass tumblers and the flip of cards,
To feel protected from the night outside:
Safe Cornish holidays before the storm!

HISTORY

*Laurence
Binyon*

Time has stored all, but keeps his chronicle
In secret, beyond all our probe or gauge.
There flows the human story, vast and full;
And here a muddy trickle smears the page.

The things our hearts remember make a sound
So faint; so loud the menace and applause.
The gleaners come, with eyes upon the ground
After Oblivion's harvest, picking straws.

What is man, if this only has told his tale,
For whom ruin and blunder mark the years,
Whom continent-shadowing conquerors regale
To surfeiting, with glory of blood and tears?

He flaunts his folly and woe in a proud dress:
But writes no history of his happiness.

THE BURNING OF THE LEAVES

Now is the time for the burning of the leaves.
They go to the fire; the nostril pricks with smoke
Wandering slowly into a weeping mist.
Brittle and blotched, ragged and rotten sheaves!
A flame seizes the smouldering ruin and bites
On stubborn stalks that crackle as they resist.

The last hollyhock's fallen tower is dust;
All the spices of June are a bitter reek,
All the extravagant riches spent and mean.
All burns! The reddest rose is a ghost;
Sparks whirl up, to expire in the mist: the wild
Fingers of fire are making corruption clean.

Now is the time for stripping the spirit bare,
Time for the burning of days ended and done,
Idle solace of things that have gone before:
Rootless hope and fruitless desire are there;
Let them go to the fire with never a look behind.
That world that was ours is a world that is ours no more.

They will come again, the leaf and the flower, to arise
From squalor of rottenness into the old splendour,
And magical scents to a wondering memory bring;
The same glory, to shine upon different eyes.
Earth cares for her own ruins, naught for ours.
Nothing is certain, only the certain spring.

THE PIKE

From shadows of rich oaks outpeer
The moss-green bastions of the weir,
   Where the quick dipper forages
   In elver-peopled crevices,
And a small runlet trickling down the sluice
Gossamer music tires not to unloose,

   Else round the broad pool's hush
      Nothing stirs,
Unless sometime a straggling heifer crush
Through the thronged spinney whence the pheasant whirs;
   Or martins in a flash
Come with wild mirth to dip their magical wings,
While in the shallow some doomed bulrush swings
   At whose hid root the diver vole's teeth gnash.

And nigh this toppling reed, still as the dead
   The great pike lies, the murderous patriarch,
   Watching the waterpit shelving and dark,
Where through the plash his lithe bright vassals thread.

   The rose-finned roach and bluish bream
   And staring ruffe steal up the stream
   Hard by their glutted tyrant, now
      Still as a sunken bough.

      He on the sandbank lies,
         Sunning himself long hours
      With stony gorgon eyes:
         Westward the hot sun lowers.

Edmund
Blunden

21

Sudden the grey pike changes, and quivering, poises for slaughter;
Intense terror wakens around him, the shoals scud awry, but there
chances
A chub unsuspecting; the prowling fins quicken, in fury he lances;
And the miller that opens the hatch stands amazed at the whirl in the
water.

BROOK IN DROUGHT

The willow catkins fall on the muddy pool
Churned up anew by cows who came to cool:
And under shoal the sticklebacks, to whom
The infant stream is like the whale's searoom,
Or Amazon to a cayman; wondering there,
They rise and thrilling sip that strange sharp Air.
The plunging stone down from the dwarf bridge thrown
Is Zeus's bolt—Zeus shambles whistling on,
And from their puny caverns they are seen
Returning where the high god's wrath has been.

Meantime a god indeed with fierce desire
Drinks of their lessening waters, tongued with fire;
He all along the willows' silver line
Diminishes the pools that pleased the kine,
And in a day will strew with tiny bones
This universe dried into sands and stones.

BELLS

What master singer, with what glory amazed,
Heard one day listening on the lonely air
The tune of bells ere yet a bell was raised
To throne it over field and flood? Who dare
Deny him demi-god, that so could win
The music uncreate, that so could wed
Music and hue—till, when the bells begin,
Song colours, colour sings? Beauty so bred
Enspheres each hamlet through the English shires,
And utters from ten thousand peeping spires
(Or huge in starlight) to the outmost farms
Sweet, young, grand, old. The country's lustiest arms
Leap to the time till the whole sky retells
That unknown poet's masterpiece of bells.

TRIUMPH OF AUTUMN

I see your signal, and the lands have seen,
And are prepared. Your hour, your fortune. Ride
More boldly then where none can intervene,
Not now in some pale bough or low mist hide.
With conquest occupy your splendid scene,
Throng the fantastic tourneyings of your pride.
Your hour, your fortune. Undisguise your will
And try your genius, king, from bannered grove to golden hill.

Vast is the triumph which at your behest
Will blaze abroad. The sun himself shall stride
With clanging pomp, bronze east to rubied west,
The moon sway wine-flushed after, lion-eyed
Star-companies form, tree-columns of glittering crest
Uphold their rank in blue air, strong and wide
Rivers go wheeling through enormous plains,
Forests assume the purple, harvests roll their rumbling wains.

Meanwhile let no one whisper time's plain fact,
Or hint an embered ending. Leaves that sighed
In falling syllabled no wrath. The stacked
And vatted yield of the year has not denied
This cloth of gold. The church clock told exact
Moment on moment gone, but only plied
His task in the general show and with gilt hand
Paid compliment, meant nothing but a child may understand.

Who cannot now be glad with even the least
Of the pageant? Here the pear tree warped and dried,
There cob suspected barren, brings brave feast,
Bright apples lantern the earlier eventide.
With elder, hop, crab, blackberry, sloe increased
To swell your flame each straggling hedge has tried,
Great season; sunflowers clamber atop each fence,
Flaring salute, each aster like his master beams immense.

These in the margin of the world-wide page
Whereof you paint the midst, these orbed and pied
Delay the eye that you would wholly engage
With your own sanguine colours. Light airs glide
About your streamered car, your travelling cage.
They were but perfume wafting, and they died.
But some tell me they hear them gathering power
Until with ocean voice they sound the extinction of your hour.

THE MIDNIGHT SKATERS

Edmund
Blunden

The hop-poles stand in cones,
　　The icy pond lurks under,
The pole-tops steeple to the thrones
　　Of stars, sound gulfs of wonder;
But not the tallest there, 'tis said,
Could fathom to this pond's black bed.

Then is not death at watch
　　Within those secret waters?
What wants he but to catch
　　Earth's heedless sons and daughters?
With but a crystal parapet
Between, he has his engines set.

Then on, blood shouts, on, on,
　　Twirl, wheel and whip above him,
Dance on this ball-floor thin and wan,
　　Use him as though you love him;
Court him, elude him, reel and pass,
And let him hate you through the glass.

THE GIANT PUFFBALL

From what proud star I know not, but I found
Myself newborn below the coppice rail,
No bigger than the dewdrops and as round,
In a soft sward, no cattle might assail.

And here I gathered mightiness and grew
With this one dream kindling in me: that I
Should never cease from conquering light and dew
Till my white splendour touched the trembling sky.

A century of blue and stilly light
Bowed down before me, the dew came agen,
The moon my sibyl worshipped through the night,
The sun returned and long revered: but then

Hoarse drooping darkness hung me with a shroud
And switched at me with shrivelled leaves in scorn:
Red morning stole beneath a grinning cloud,
And suddenly clambering over dike and thorn

A half-moon host of churls with flags and sticks
Hallooed and hurtled up the partridge brood,
And Death clapped hands from all the echoing thicks,
And trampling envy spied me where I stood;

Who haled me tired and quaking, hid me by,
And came agen after an age of cold,
And hung me in the prison-house a-dry
From the great crossbeam. Here defiled and old

I perish through unnumbered hours, I swoon,
Hacked with harsh knives to staunch a child's torn hand;
And all my hopes must with my body soon
Be but as crouching dust and wind-blown sand.

DEPARTED
or, 'tis more than twenty years since

Moated and granged, recall the Gentry who
Could as they would, but never wrongly, do;
These at their wedding paid for anthem sung,
For voluntary played, and rice unflung.
Their funeral also had its golden tint,
Our choristers confused it with the Mint:
On the sad day, Regret would reign at three,
And later came Rejoicing with the fee.
To Gentry and no others was assigned
This special power: they in the evening dined.
Their cricket caps, of floral stripe and dye,
Proclaimed accomplishment, and did not lie.
For them a pitch smooth as their bowling-screen
Was guarded from the rougher, dustier green.
In church their knees impressed soft hassocks; they
At mattins came, at vespers were away,
Except that spinster whose kind cherubs flew
About her while she moved from pew to pew
Lighting the candles. Parrots, mourn your friend!
Canaries, let your trills to her ascend!

*   *   *

Who now succeed? What demigods have we?
Who scraped the gilding from the family tree?
Ask of the roadhouse, try the bungalow.
Welcome, Squire Thenks-Chum and Lord Arfamo.

POLAND, OCTOBER

Charles
Brasch

Even for the defeated life goes on,
Although the codes, assumptions, purposes
That guided and protected them are gone:
They have become the prey of nothingness.

All that was and was known now only seems,
All seeming changes and all change appals,
As they live out the intolerable dreams
That usurp nature to itself grown false.

They have been used and are not wanted any more,
Not by man; they will not be pitied nor
Remembered. Only to suffer are they still free.
Pain can practise new experiments on them,
Until the fair-spoken world their lives condemn
Dies in each one's death. They are history.

GREY OWL

Joseph Payne
Brennan

When fireflies begin to wink
over the stubble near the wood,
ghost-of-the-air,
the grey owl, glides into dusk

Over the spruce, a drift of smoke,
over the juniper knoll,
whispering wings
making the sound of silk unfurling,
in the soft blur of starlight
a puff of feathers blown about.

Terrible fixed eyes,
talons sheathed in down,
refute this floating wraith.

Before the shapes of mist
show white beneath the moon,
the rabbit or the rat
will know the knives of fire,
the pothooks swinging out of space.

26

But now the muffled hunter
moves like smoke, like wind,
scarcely apprehended,
barely glimpsed and gone,
like a grey thought
fanning the margins of the mind.

THE CHURCH MOUSE

Here in a crumbled corner of the wall,

Gerald
Bullett

Well stockt with food from harvest festival,
My twitching ears and delicate small snout
And velvet feet that know their way about
From age to age in snug contentment dwell,
Unseen, and serve my hungry nestlings well.

The slanting light makes patterns on the floor
Of nave and chancel. At my kitchen door
God's acre stretches greenly, should I wish
To take the air and seek a daintier dish.
And week by week the shuddering organ mews,
And all my world is filled with boots and shoes.

Sometimes, on Sundays, from my living tomb
I venture out into the vast room,
Smelling my way, as pious as you please,
Among the hassocks and the bended knees,
To join with giants, being filled with food,
In worship of the Beautiful, the Good:
The all-creative Incorporeal Mouse,
Whose radiant odours warm this holy house.

FINAL STONE

No giant walks the final land,

Jean
Burden

no mountain towers, no wall;
no leviathan of sea or mind
withstands the brutal sifting of the tide.

27

What we live by in the end
is polished for the hand,
purified,
and small.

Final word and ultimate stone
lie on the sea's floor
with the grains of hills
and the shark's tooth
and the small ear-bones of whales.

MEN IN GREEN

*David
Campbell*

Oh, there were fifteen men in green,
Each with a tommy-gun,
Who leapt into my plane at dawn;
We rose to meet the sun.

We set our course towards the east
And climbed into the day
Till the ribbed jungle underneath
Like a giant fossil lay.

We climbed towards the distant range
Where two white paws of cloud
Clutched at the shoulders of the pass;
The green men laughed aloud.

They did not fear the ape-like cloud
That climbed the mountain crest
And hung from twisted ropes of air
With thunder in their breast.

They did not fear the summer's sun,
In whose hot centre lie
A hundred hissing cannon shells
For the unwatchful eye.

And when on Dobadura's field
We landed, each man raised
His thumb towards the open sky;
But to their right I gazed.

For fifteen men in jungle green
Rose from the kunai grass
And came towards the plane. My men
In silence watched them pass;
It seemed they looked upon themselves
In Time's prophetic glass.

Oh, there were some leaned on a stick
And some on stretchers lay,
But few walked on their own two feet
In the early green of day.

They had not feared the ape-like cloud
That climbed the mountain crest;
They had not feared the summer's sun
With bullets for their breast.

Their eyes were bright, their looks were dull,
Their skin had turned to clay.
Nature had met them in the night
And stalked them in the day.

And I think still of men in green
On the Soputa track
With fifteen spitting tommy-guns
To keep a jungle back.

THE THEOLOGY OF BONGWI, THE BABOON

This is the wisdom of the Ape
  Who yelps beneath the Moon—
'Tis God who made me in His shape
  He is a Great Baboon.
'Tis He who tilts the moon askew
  And fans the forest trees,
The heavens which are broad and blue
  Provide him his trapeze;
He swings with tail divinely bent
  Around those azure bars
And munches to his Soul's content
  The kernels of the stars;
And when I die, His loving care
  Will raise me from the sod
To learn the perfect Mischief there,
  The Nimbleness of God.

Roy Campbell

THE SERF

Roy
Campbell

His naked skin clothed in the torrid mist
That puffs in smoke around the patient hooves,
The ploughman drives, a slow somnambulist,
And through the green his crimson furrow grooves.
His heart, more deeply than he wounds the plain,
Long by the rasping share of insult torn,
Red clod, to which the war-cry once was rain
And tribal spears the fatal sheaves of corn,
Lies fallow now. But as the turf divides
I see in the slow progress of his strides
Over the toppled clods and falling flowers,
The timeless, surly patience of the serf
That moves the nearest to the naked earth
And ploughs down palaces, and thrones, and towers.

AUTUMN

I love to see, when leaves depart,
The clear anatomy arrive,
Winter, the paragon of art,
That kills all forms of life and feeling
Save what is pure and will survive.

Already now the clanging chains
Of geese are harnessed to the moon:
Stripped are the great sun-clouding planes:
And the dark pines, their own revealing,
Let in the needles of the noon.

Strained by the gale the olives whiten
Like hoary wrestlers bent with toil
And, with the vines, their branches lighten
To brim our vats where summer lingers
In the red froth and sun-gold oil.

Soon on our hearth's reviving pyre
Their rotted stems will crumble up:
And like a ruby, panting fire,
The grape will redden on your fingers
Through the lit crystal of the cup.

AFRICAN MOONRISE
To Tony Van den Bergh

The wind with foetid muzzle sniffed its feast,
The carrion town, that lulled its crowds to rest
Like the sprawled carcase of some giant beast
That hives the rustling larvae in its breast.

When the cold moon rose glinting from the fen
And snailed her slime of fire along the hill,
Insomnia, the Muse of angry men,
To other themes had chid my faithless quill.

But wide I flung the shutters on their hinges
And watched the moon as from the gilded mire
Where the black river trails its reedy fringes,
She fished her shadow with a line of fire.

Against her light the dusty palms were charred:
The frogs, her faithless troubadours, were still,
Alone, it seemed, I kept my trusty guard
Over the stone-grey silence of the hill,

Till a starved mongrel tugging at his chain
With fearful jerks, hairless and wide of eye,
From where he crouched, a thrilling spear of pain,
Hurled forth his Alleluia to the sky.

Fierce tremors volted through his bony notches
And shook the skirling bag-pipe of his hide—
Beauty has still one faithful heart who watches,
One last Endymion left to hymn her pride!

Sing on, lone voice! make all the desert ring,
My listening spirit kindles and adores . . .
Such were my voice, had I the heart to sing,
But mine should be a fiercer howl than yours!

WASHING DAY

Amongst the rooftop chimneys where the breezes
Their dizzy choreography design,
Pyjamas, combinations, and chemises
Inflate themselves and dance upon the line.

31

Drilled by a loose disorder and abandon,
They belly and explode, revolve and swing,
As fearless of the precipice they stand on
As if there were religion in a string.
Annexing with their parachute invasion
The intimate behaviour of our life,
They argue, or embrace with kind persuasion,
And parody our dalliance or our strife.
We change ideas and moods like shirts or singlets,
Which, having shed, they rise to mock us still:
And the wind laughs and shakes her golden ringlets
To set them independent of our will.
They curtsey and collapse, revolve and billow—
A warning that, when least aware we lie,
The dreams are incubated in our pillow
That animate its chrysalis to fly.

ARCHAEOLOGY

Richard
Church

They say a church once stood in this Anglian field.
But there's no village here it could have served.
The district is a plateau, wide and wild,
Where winds meet, and scrub-bush only has thrived
For centuries, except on one lonely farm.

Here in its acres set grim and taciturn,
An outpost of humanity, it holds
Authority of a field or two; no more.
The wind is master here, and grudgingly yields
A yearly crop of corn, too thin for flour.

But in the early summer, when the tyrant
Relents for a month, and growing lenient
Breaks into bramble-flowers, and eglantine,
And all the little outlaws man dismisses
From garden beds and honestly hoed fields,
Then the dim murmurs of old homes, and guesses
About a church once sanctifying these wilds,
Are proved in barley. Where it rises green
A deeper hue of tall blades, cruciform,
Reveals the old foundations. No need to search
By gossip or legend. There stands the living church.

SMALL MERCIES, 1934

Three years have gone since I looked down
From ridge of rock and snow
To Freiburg jewelled on the plain
Four thousand feet below.

But I can smell the icy air,
And hear my voice ring out
With mountain clearness like a flame
That time still blows about.

If sight, sound, smell can thus survive
Thought's slow, corrosive greed,
I'll keep my faith in senses five,
And scorn a greater need.

HOUSING SCHEME

All summer through
The field drank showers of larksong;
Offering in return
The hospitality of grasses,
And flowers kneedeep.

Over those wide acres
Trooped the plovers,
Mourning and lamenting as evening fell.
From the deep hedgerows
Where the foam of meadowsweet broke,
The rabbits and mice
Peeped out, and boldly sat in the sun.

But when the oaks were bronzing,
Steamrollers and brickcarts
Broke through the hedges.
The white-haired grasses, and the seedpods
Disappeared into the mud,
And the larks were silent, the plovers gone.

Then over the newlaid roads
And the open trenches of drains,
Rose a hoarding to face the highway,
'Build your house in the country.'

THE WARNING

Swallows still haunted the aerials and eaves;
And the billowing clouds of Michaelmas blooms
Rang with bee-traffic.
Late butterflies staggered through the low sunbeams,
Lingering under their drowsy warmth.
All the world was green and sedate,
No fever in the beeches, no fire in the elms.

Not until the sun
Had slipped quietly, too quickly, down the evening,
Did treachery show its cold hand.

Not the glowworm
In her grassy vault;
Not the moonlight
Weighing on the foliage and heavy fans of the trees,
And dwarfing the distant hills;
Not in these lay the foreboding.

But in that glitter of stars,
And shrinking of the air,
The teeth of death
Proffered their kiss.

PICCADILLY PASTORAL

Walking along the pavements in the rain,
I thought of summer, and the ripened grain
Rolling its golden billows in the lowland valley.
I heard above the dun rain and the din,
Lazy yellowhammers in the whin.
And I snuffed the scent of apples in the wet brick alley.

Yes, I saw 'buses come ambling down the hill
Coming to be milked at the call of Jane and Jill.
And the rabbits in the Circus where the hollow theatres stand
Were hurrying and scurrying across the thistled land.
Brown bracken, whose salt scent is borrowed from the sea,
Sighed with the passing traffic, and swung the resting bee.
Mingled with the uproar of the motor-vans and taxis,
I heard the falling timber, and the crash of woodmen's axes;
While basking on the green leaves of the Piccadilly clubs,
Fed greedy caterpillars, and fat and shining grubs.

THE VISITOR

'If Beauty calls, my door
Shall be unlatched', said I.
And Beauty came—a gay,
A carefree visitor.

Pleased with her witching ways,
I played the host. But now
I find that I must go,
While Beauty, smiling, stays.

Henry
Compton

STEEL

There have been times when I could have accepted steel.
Looking at plough-shares in the corners of cart-sheds
Or at square-headed nails studding the riven oak
Of the chests and doors of ancient churches,
I have seen friendly flames deep in a dim smithy,
Warming its heart, as the declining sun
Mellows November mists on Midland fields—
And I have believed that Vulcan loved, like men.

But when I see the imbecility of motor bicycles,
The sleek fatuity of motor cars,
The unholy precision of machine guns,
And the hollow pretensions of tanks,
I behold hell (which is like Sheffield)
And the outer darkness (which is like Birmingham),
With devils feeding the fiercely mocking flames,
Deep in impenetrable night,
And the arch-fiend seaming earth with ore
To wither and harden souls, else saved.

Therefore I fear that this corruptible iron
Shall never put on incorruption,
Nor even decay serenely
Like old men and old walls beneath the sun,
But, rusting, turn battle's honour into junk.
And therefore my heart declares:
The delicate lancet cannot justify
The bullet blundering through flesh,
Metallic wings, though multi-engined, cannot lift
Iron that has entered into the soul,
The body cannot breed
From the automaton.

Must they who touch pitch be defiled?—
I ask and cannot answer.
Now I know only this:
That I must grip the indifferent lever with an eager hand,
Hold firm the rasp that files the fineness of the mind,
Work poisoned ore, more bitter even than gold,
And whisper to the blighted, blind and palsied night
My hope of lifting clean hands to the dawn.

IMMORTALITY

These fields, which now lie smiling in the sun,
Were tamed and schooled to harvest long ago
By men whose lives, whose names, we cannot know,
Who went in silence when their work was done.

Their furrows, slowly traced, their crops, hard⁄won,
Have vanished like some ancient winter's snow,
Their hearts, dispersed in dust, have ceased to glow,
Mere random bones declare their race is run.

And yet within the fields there lie in wait
Strange virtues which to them, not us, belong,
And as we plod behind the plough which bares
The gracious earth they wooed, we know the strong
Compulsion laid by them on all their heirs,
And cannot choose but drive our furrows straight.

TRAVELLING HOME

Frances
Cornford

The train. A hot July. On either hand
Our sober, fruitful, unemphatic land,
This Cambridge country plain beneath the sky
Where I was born, and grew, and hope to die.

Look! where the willows hide a rushy pool,
And the old horse goes squelching down to cool,
One angler's rod against their silvery green,
Still seen today as once by Bewick seen.

A cottage there, thatched sadly, like its earth,
Where crimson ramblers make a shortlived mirth;
Here, only flies the flick⁄tail cows disturb
Among the shaven meads and willow⁄herb.

36

There, rounded hay-ricks solemn in the yard,
Barns gravely, puritanically tarred,
Next heavy elms that guard the ripening grain
And fields, and elms, and corn, and fields again.

Over the soft savannahs of the corn,
Like ships the hot white butterflies are borne,
While clouds pass slowly on the flower-blue dome
Like spirits in a vast and peaceful home.

Over the Dyke I watch their shadows flow
As the Icenian watched them long ago;
So let me in this Cambridge calm July
Fruitfully live and undistinguished die.

'ANYONE LIVED IN A PRETTY HOW TOWN'

anyone lived in a pretty how town   *E. E. Cummings*
(with up so floating many bells down)
spring summer autumn winter
he sang his didn't he danced his did.

Women and men(both little and small)
cared for anyone not at all
they sowed their isn't they reaped their same
sun moon stars rain

children guessed(but only a few
and down they forgot as up they grew
autumn winter spring summer)
that noone loved him more by more

when by now and tree by leaf
she laughed his joy she cried his grief
bird by snow and stir by still
anyone's any was all to her

someones married their everyones
laughed their cryings and did their dance
(sleep wake hope and then)they
said their nevers they slept their dream

stars rain sun moon
(and only the snow can begin to explain
how children are apt to forget to remember
with up so floating many bells down)

one day anyone died i guess
(and noone stooped to kiss his face)
busy folk buried them side by side
little by little and was by was

all by all and deep by deep
and more by more they dream their sleep
noone and anyone earth by april
wish by spirit and if by yes.

Women and men(both dong and ding)
summer autumn winter spring
reaped their sowing and went their came
sun moon stars rain

'IN JUST'

in Just⁄
spring   when the world is mud⁄
luscious the little
lame balloonman

whistles   far   and wee

and eddieandbill come
running from marbles and
piracies and it's
spring

when the world is puddle⁄wonderful

the queer
old balloonman whistles
far   and   wee
and bettyandisbel come dancing

from hop⁄scotch and jump⁄rope and

it's
spring
and
    the

        goat⁄footed

balloonMan   whistles
far
and
wee

'WHAT IF A MUCH OF A WHICH OF A WIND'

what if a much of a which of a wind
gives the truth to summer's lie;
bloodies with dizzying leaves the sun
and yanks immortal stars awry?
Blow king to beggar and queen to seem
(blow friend to fiend:blow space to time)
—when skies are hanged and oceans drowned,
the single secret will still be man

what if a keen of a lean wind flays
screaming hills with sleet and snow:
strangles valleys by ropes of thing
and stifles forests in white ago?
Blow hope to terror;blow seeing to blind
(blow pity to envy and soul to mind)
—whose hearts are mountains,roots are trees,
it's they shall cry hello to the spring

what if a dawn of a doom of a dream
bites this universe in two,
peels forever out of his grave
and sprinkles nowhere with me and you?
Blow soon to never and never to twice
(blow life to isn't:blow death to was)
—all nothing's only our hugest home;
the most who die,the more we live

'SPRING IS LIKE A PERHAPS HAND'

Spring is like a perhaps hand
(which comes carefully
out of Nowhere)arranging
a window,into which people look(while
people stare
arranging and changing placing
carefully there a strange
thing and a known thing here)and

changing everything carefully

spring is like a perhaps
Hand in a window
(carefully to
and fro moving New and
Old things,while
people stare carefully
moving a perhaps
fraction of flower here placing
an inch of air there)and

without breaking anything.

LAMENT FOR A SAILOR

Paul Dehn

Here, where the night is clear as sea-water
And stones are white and the sticks are spars,
Swims on a windless, mackerel tide
The dolphin moon in a shoal of stars.

Here, in the limbo, where moths are spinners
And clouds like hulls drift overhead,
Move we must for our colder comfort,
I the living and you the dead.

Each on our way, my ghost, my grayling.
You to the water, the land for me;
I am the fat-knuckled, noisy diver
But you are the quietest fish in the sea.

SOLITUDE

*Walter
de la Mare*

When the high road
Forks into a by-road,
And that drifts into a lane,
And the lane breaks into a bridle-path,
A chace forgotten
Still as death,
And green with the long night's rain;
Through a forest winding on and on,
Moss, and fern, and sun-bleached bone,
Till only a trace remain;

And that dies out in a waste of stone
A bluff of cliff, vast, trackless, wild,
Blue with the harebell, undefiled;
Where silence enthralls the empty air,
Mute with a presence unearthly fair,
        And a path is sought
           In vain. . . . .

      It is then the Ocean
      Looms into sight,
A gulf enringed with a burning white,
A sea of sapphire, dazzling bright;
      And islands,
    Peaks of such beauty that
Bright danger seems to lie in wait,
Dread, disaster, boding fate;
And soul and sense are appalled thereat;
Though an Ariel music on the breeze
Thrills the mind with a lorn unease,
Cold with all mortal mysteries.
        And every thorn,
        And weed, and flower,
     And every time-worn stone
A challenge cries on the trespasser:
        Beware!
        Thou art alone!

TARBURY STEEP

The moon in her gold over Tarbury Steep
  Wheeled full, in the hush of the night,
To rabbit and hare she gave her chill beams
  And to me on that silvery height.

From the dusk of its glens thrilled the nightjar's strange cry,
  A peewit wailed over the wheat,
Else still was the air, though the stars in the sky
  Seemed with music in beauty to beat.

O many a mortal has sat there before,
  Since its chalk lay in shells in the sea,
And the ghosts that looked out of the eyes of them all
  Shared Tarbury's moonlight with me.

And many, as transient, when I have gone down,
  To the shades and the silence of sleep,
Will gaze, lost in dream, on the loveliness seen
  In the moonshine of Tarbury Steep.

THE LAST GUEST

Now that thy friends are gone,
  And the spent candles, one by one,
Thin out their smoke upon the darkening air;
  Now that the feast's first flowers
Flagged have irrevocably in these latening hours,
With perfumes that but tell how sweet they were;
  Turn now—the door ajar—
  See, there, thy winter star,
Amid its wheeling consorts wildly bright,
Herald of inward rapture, never of rest!
Still must thy threshold wait a laggard guest
  Who comes, alone, by night.

FRESCOES IN AN OLD CHURCH

Six centuries now have gone
Since, one by one,
These stones were laid,
And in air's vacancy
This beauty made.

They who thus reared them
Their long rest have won;
Ours now this heritage—
To guard, preserve, delight in, brood upon;
And in these transitory fragments scan
The immortal longings in the soul of Man.

MEMORY

When summer heat has drowsed the day
With blaze of noontide overhead,
And hidden greenfinch can but say
What but a moment since it said;
When harvest fields stand thick with wheat,
And wasp and bee slave—dawn till dark—

Nor home, till evening moonbeams beat,
Silvering the nightjar's oaken bark;
How strangely then the mind may build
A magic world of wintry cold,
Its meadows with frail frost-flowers filled—
Bright-ribbed with ice, a frozen wold! . . .

When dusk shuts in the shortest day,
And huge Orion spans the night;
Where antlered fireflames leap and play
Chequering the walls with fitful light—
Even sweeter in mind the summer's rose
May bloom again; her drifting swan
Resume her beauty; while rapture flows
Of birds long since to silence gone:
Beyond the Nowel, sharp and shrill,
Of Waits from out the snowbound street,
Drums to their fiddle beneath the hill
June's mill wheel where the waters meet . . .

O angel Memory that can
Double the joys of faithless Man!

MORTALITY

The lone watch of the moon over mountains old.
Night that is never silent, and none to hark.
Down in the inky pool a fish leaps
With splash of silver light in the liquid dark.

I walk the unknown ways of a foreign land.
The close reeds whisper their secrecies,
And hidden water tunes—earth's oldest voice.
What alien waif is mind among mindless these?

Old, old, everything here is old.
Life the intruder but so briefly stays,
And man the dreamer—soon old changeless time
Will grass his ways.

Fold him, spade him away. Where are they now,
The high courage and love, the laboured store?
Down in the inky pool a fish leapt—
Life is no more.

*James
Devaney*

NASEBY: LATE AUTUMN

Basil
Dowling

Larches about this retrospective town
Display their gold not laboured at nor spun.
But in this man-made chasm, yellow-brown,
A wiry miner elbow-numb with cold
Gumbooted stands and with his swivel gun
Boils down whole hillsides for a different gold
More loved than autumn larch, gorse bloom, or sun.
Fierce water with incessant soft explosion
Bores and devours and sifts rich clay from stone,
Divorcing with its terrible erosion
The body of earth from fundamental bone.

Sly gold eludes my fumblings with a dish
Until experience, with tilt and swish,
Cradles and coaxes out each shiny flake.
So satisfied I stumble down the slope
By mustard creek and small sky-gazing lake
Musing on man and mineral, and take
This gleam of greed home in an envelope.

CONTRAST

Eileen
Duggan

It was so cold the skyline seemed to splinter
As the ice in the puddles cracked beneath the camels.
The great statute that we know as winter,
Unsoftened yet by any Spring amendment,
Was full enforced—a sumptuary law,
Forbidding earth undue indulgence
In leaf and flower, in hip and haw.

The caravan swayed like a ship under canvas when its topsails belly
   in the wind,
And the Magi looked over the rolling dunes
As a sailor to shore in his mind.
Their light in the dusk was like a lantern at a mast-head,
Seen dipping, the bluer for the salt air, afar off;
And their thought was deep and slow and undulating
Like the rising and falling of a galley in the sea's trough—
All very leisurely as demand great distances—
And the star, as slow as reason, undulated too.

44

Ah but the shepherds on the hill above the grotto,
Like a bolt from the blue,
Hurtled headlong, helter-skelter, wild-foot, down the cragside,
As fast as instinct—no conjecture, no dismay!
They had not watched for years; they had not calculated;
But they knew the way.

THE AXE IN THE WOOD

I stopped to watch a man strike at the trunk
Of a tree grown strong through many centuries.
His quick axe, sharp and glittering, struck deep,
And yellow chips went spinning in the air—
And I remember how I liked the sight
Of poise and rhythm as the bright axe swung.
A man who fells a tree makes people watch:
A swinging axe has always drawn a crowd.

I know the answers to the chanced reproach:
How old the tree was, and how dangerous,
How it might fall, how timber in a stack
Had more good in it than a growing tree—
But I saw death cut down a thousand men
In that tall lovely legacy of wood.

*Clifford
Dyment*

THE WINTER TREES

Against the evening sky the trees are black,
Iron themselves against the iron rails;
The hurrying crowds seek cinemas or homes,
Some cosy hour where warmth will mock the wind.
They do not look at trees now summer's gone,
For fallen with their leaves are those glad days
Of sand and sea and ships, of swallows, lambs,
Of cricket teams, and walking long in woods.

Standing among the trees, a shadow bends
And picks a cigarette-end from the ground;
It lifts the collar of an overcoat,
And blows upon its hands and stamps its feet—
For this is winter, whip for the innocent,
This is the winter, season of closed hands.

THE WAYFARER

A lamp shines in a single window,
And the wayfarer pauses, looks ahead.

The fields not mute now, though the sensitive fabric
Of a man's ear must be taut and tuned
To register the rub of a vole's red body
Against a bush; the crack of the mouse's skull
In an owl's beak; the badger's and the rabbit's way;
The wind winding among the stems of flowers,
And a leaf falling on the grass.

The fields not mute, though the sounds are small,
And in nocturnal quiet lost.
The huge wood whispering,
The invisible hills somewhere to the south,
And the city far away
Are covered by the wide hand of the sky,
The hand that is freckled with stars.

The wayfarer, standing in the enormous meadow,
Sees the yellow square of the lamp
And knows the fox is not his brother,
Nor the drifting owl his guide;
Knows the stone no pillow, nor soil his bread,
Nor the milk of petals his wine.
Looking ahead, the wayfarer knows this,
And is aware that he must kneel
To know the creatures whom he loves,
For the wayfarer is solitary in his country.

BURDEN

Richard
Eberhart

Whoever lives beside a mountain knows,
Although he dares not speak it out, that he
Must always carry on his heart the snows
That burden down the trees. And never the sea
Will rush around him cool, like snow-cool air,
And carry him and lift him like a leaf.
He will not find this lightness anywhere
Since mountains brood, they hold dark league with grief.

46

The pine trees never tire of moving down
The slopes to meet him, pointing up from town
Beyond the tree-line to the rigid peaks.
The mountain holds him though it never speaks.
He scrambles over boulders on his knees
Trying to reach the summit, like the trees.

JOURNEY OF THE MAGI

'A cold coming we had of it,   *T. S. Eliot*
Just the worst time of the year
For a journey, and such a long journey:
The ways deep and the weather sharp,
The very dead of winter.'
And the camels galled, sore-footed, refractory,
Lying down in the melting snow.
There were times we regretted
The summer palaces on slopes, the terraces,
And the silken girls bringing sherbet.
Then the camel men cursing and grumbling
And running away, and wanting their liquor and women,
And the night-fires going out, and the lack of shelters,
And the cities hostile and the towns unfriendly
And the villages dirty and charging high prices:
A hard time we had of it.
At the end we preferred to travel all night,
Sleeping in snatches,
With the voices singing in our ears, saying
That this was all folly.

Then at dawn we came down to a temperate valley,
Wet, below the snow line, smelling of vegetation;
With a running stream and a water-mill beating the darkness,
And three trees on the low sky,
And an old white horse galloped away in the meadow.
Then we came to a tavern with vine-leaves over the lintel,
Six hands at an open door dicing for pieces of silver,
And feet kicking the empty wine-skins.
But there was no information, and so we continued
And arrived at evening, not a moment too soon
Finding the place; it was (you may say) satisfactory.

T. S. Eliot   All this was a long time ago, I remember,
And I would do it again, but set down
This set down
This: were we led all that way for
Birth or Death? There was a Birth, certainly,
We had evidence and no doubt. I had seen birth and death,
But had thought they were different; this Birth was
Hard and bitter agony for us, like Death, our Death.
We returned to our places, these Kingdoms,
But no longer at ease here, in the old dispensation,
With an alien people clutching their gods.
I should be glad of another death.

From 'THE DRY SALVAGES'

I do not know much about gods; but I think that the river
Is a strong brown god—sullen, untamed and intractable,
Patient to some degree, at first recognised as a frontier;
Useful, untrustworthy, as a conveyor of commerce;
Then only a problem confronting the builder of bridges.
The problem once solved, the brown god is almost forgotten
By the dwellers in cities—ever, however, implacable,
Keeping his seasons and rages, destroyer, reminder
Of what men choose to forget. Unhonoured, unpropitiated
By worshippers of the machine, but waiting, watching and waiting.
His rhythm was present in the nursery bedroom,
In the rank ailanthus of the April dooryard,
In the smell of grapes on the autumn table,
And the evening circle in the winter gaslight.

The river is within us, the sea is all about us;
The sea is the land's edge also, the granite
Into which it reaches, the beaches where it tosses
Its hints of earlier and other creation:
The starfish, the horseshoe crab, the whale's backbone;
The pools where it offers to our curiosity
The more delicate algae and the sea anemone.
It tosses up our losses, the torn seine,
The shattered lobsterpot. the broken oar
And the gear of foreign dead men. The sea has many voices,
Many gods and many voices.
                    The salt is on the briar rose,
The fog is in the fir trees.

The sea howl
And the sea yelp, are different voices
Often together heard: the whine in the rigging,
The menace and caress of wave that breaks on water,
The distant rote in the granite teeth,
And the wailing warning from the approaching headland
Are all sea voices, and the heaving groaner
Rounded homewards, and the seagull:
And under the oppression of the silent fog
The tolling bell
Measures time not our time, rung by the unhurried
Ground swell, a time
Older than the time of chronometers, older
Than time counted by anxious worried women
Lying awake, calculating the future,
Trying to unweave, unwind, unravel
And piece together the past and the future
Between midnight and dawn, when the past is all deception,
The future futureless, before the morning watch
When time stops and time is never ending;
And the ground swell, that is and was from the beginning,
Clangs
The bell.

CHORUS from 'THE ROCK'

The Eagle soars in the summit of Heaven,
The Hunter with his dogs pursues his circuit.
O perpetual revolution of configured stars,
O perpetual recurrence of determined seasons,
O world of spring and autumn, birth and dying!
The endless cycle of idea and action,
Endless invention, endless experiment,
Brings knowledge of motion, but not of stillness;
Knowledge of speech, but not of silence;
Knowledge of words, and ignorance of the Word.
All our knowledge brings us nearer to our ignorance,
All our ignorance brings us nearer to death,
But nearness to death no nearer to GOD.
Where is the Life we have lost in living?
Where is the wisdom we have lost in knowledge?
Where is the knowledge we have lost in information?
The cycles of Heaven in twenty centuries
Bring us farther from GOD and nearer to the Dust.

49

I journeyed to London, to the timekept City,
Where the River flows, with foreign flotations.
There I was told: we have too many churches,
And too few chop-houses. There I was told:
Let the vicars retire. Men do not need the Church
In the place where they work, but where they spend their Sundays.
In the City, we need no bells:
Let them waken the suburbs.
I journeyed to the suburbs, and there I was told:
We toil for six days, on the seventh we must motor
To Hindhead, or Maidenhead.
If the weather is foul we stay at home and read the papers.
In industrial districts, there I was told
Of economic laws.
In the pleasant countryside, there it seemed
That the country now is only fit for picnics.
And the Church does not seem to be wanted
In country or in suburb; and in the town
Only for important weddings.

THE 'BLACK' COUNTRY

D. J.   'But it is not Black,' they will tell you, 'any longer, not really Black.'
Enright   And of course they have the right ideas, and are right.
       Progress is always changing colour: blushes more deeply, or now
           scowls darkly, or turns pale.

True, how can it be called Black?—with its shining cubes of metallic
           branch-groceries,
And the tin gleam of the fish saloon, tiled like a public lavatory,
Where the fried fish floats, in Sargasso seas of chips.

It is not Black, in the sense that the desert is Red
With a history of running sores, or that the grass was Green.
Not Black, as Babylon was Scarlet, or the Blood,
As violets are Violet, as Pythagoras' thigh was Golden, or corn is—
Not Black as the satin back of this black horse is Black.

So we shall call it the Grey Country, out of deference.
But Grey is slyer than Black: 'Why, I am practically White.'

NIGHT SONG

Though Time's black mountain overhangs
   the night where she's engrossed in sleep
its shadow cannot bruise my love,
   so calm she lies, she dreams so deep.

She is not hurt by what shall be,
   death stands enchanted in her eyes;
remote and lovely, a floating flower
   on the lily pool of sleep she lies.

Dream deep, my love, as in the time
   when your sweet spirit was unborn,
But rise up when the east is purple
   and dress your hair for Judgement morn.

A. R. D.
Fairburn

SONG AT SUMMER'S END

Down in the park the children play
rag-happy through the summer day
with dirty feet and freckled faces,
laughing, fighting, running races.
Dull against the smoky skies
the summer's heavy burden lies,
leaden leaves on tired trees
lacking supple limbs like these.

The skyline shows the shape of life,
tomorrow's world of sweat and strife,
fifty stacks and one grey steeple.
Down the street come factory people,
folk who used to play on swings,
dodging chores and apron-strings
to wrestle on the grass and run
barefoot with the fleeting sun.

Some of the kids are sailing boats;
the first leaf drops unheeded, floats
and dances on the muddy pond.
Shadows from the world beyond
lengthen, sprawl across the park;
day rolls onward towards the dark.
From the clock-tower, wreathed in smoke,
Time speaks gravely, stroke on stroke.

ALL THAT IS, AND CAN DELIGHT

Robert
Farren

In the numb time when foam froze
and sea-birds fed from the hand,
and fields like great grey paving-stones
hid green grass through the land;
when air rang to a cock's crow
as a glass to finger nail,
we had so long sung praise of snow
we had forgotten rain:

forgotten hued and moving things:
the huge winds that bay;
waters shaken with wild fins,
and root-and-worm-rent clay.
O frost held field and cloud and surf
with still Medusal eye,
and men's eyes saw the still, stone world,
coped with the stone of the sky.

But rain teemed then from melting skies,
and wind loosed lungs of brass;
and each man, with the first man's eyes,
saw the green of grass.
And each man sang the water's praise
and the wind's praise, and lo!
we, who forgot the rain's face,
forgot the grace of snow.

Father, remind thy sons of snow
when the hedge burns with the haw,
give, while the after-grasses grow,
the whiff of a wind like a claw;
let ice, the jewel of June's light,
storm the vein with the sun;
with ray-limbed, moon-marbling night
thrill the breath from the lung.
Make all that is, and can delight,
from every atom run.

DAYBREAK IN THE TROPICS

Yvonne
ffrench

Grey as the banks of mud on which they tilt
Their armoured heads, the alligators smile
Alternately disclosing greed and guile,
While staring at the thickly-moving silt.

And when the suffocating night has gone
Discovered by dawn in quick surprise,
They blink the shutters of their gilded eyes
And turn and plunge into the Amazon.

Feeling the sun's incendiary hand
Ignite the densely vegetated land
Parrots and brilliant parrakeets emerge;
And leaving their green palaces and domes
They scream across the forest's leafy verge
Like fugitives forsaking stricken homes.

UNHARVESTED

A scent of ripeness from over a wall.   *Robert*
And come to leave the routine road   *Frost*
And look for what had made me stall,
There sure enough was an apple tree
That had eased itself of its summer load,
And of all but its trivial foliage free,
Now breathed as light as a lady's fan.
For there there had been an apple fall
As complete as the apple had given man.
The ground was one circle of solid red.

May something go always unharvested!
May much stay out of our stated plan,
Apples or something forgotten and left,
So smelling their sweetness would be no theft.

THERE ARE ROUGHLY ZONES

We sit indoors and talk of the cold outside.
And every gust that gathers strength and heaves
Is a threat to the house. But the house has long been tried.
We think of the tree. If it never again has leaves,
We'll know, we say, that this was the night it died.
It is very far north, we admit, to have brought the peach.
What comes over a man, is it soul or mind—
That to no limits and bounds he can stay confined?
You would say his ambition was to extend the reach
Clear to the Arctic of every living kind.
Why is his nature forever so hard to teach
That though there is no fixed line between wrong and right,
There are roughly zones whose laws must be obeyed.

There is nothing much we can do for the tree tonight,
But we can't help feeling more than a little betrayed
That the northwest wind should rise to such a height
Just when the cold went down so many below.
The tree has no leaves and may never have them again.
We must wait till some months hence in the spring to know.
But if it is destined never again to grow,
It can blame this limitless trait in the hearts of men.

ACCEPTANCE

When the spent sun throws up its rays on cloud
And goes down burning into the gulf below,
No voice in nature is heard to cry aloud
At what has happened. Birds, at least, must know
It is the change to darkness in the sky.
Murmuring something quiet in her breast,
One bird begins to close a faded eye;
Or overtaken too far from his nest,
Hurrying low above the grove, some waif
Swoops just in time to his remembered tree.
At most he thinks or twitters softly, 'Safe!
Now let the night be dark for all of me.
Let the night be too dark for me to see
Into the future. Let what will be, be.'

PREFACE TO AN ANTHOLOGY

Roy
Fuller

Don't be deceived, some poems printed here
May merely illustrate the condemnation
Of the anthologist: omission were
Too vague a sign to show his detestation.

Nor has he chosen of the verse he likes
That he thinks quite the best: he aimed to prove
A theory in this volume, as one looks
On an old wife with warm complacent love.

With quiet pride he added just too few
Examples of his own successful work:
If the thing as a whole should fail he knew
There was at least one signpost in the murk.

Anthologists not always have the wit
To see it is their passion that abets
The gradual ruin of their choice: that what
Their pages fail to stale history forgets.

THE SNOW

The morning of the snow I walked alone
Through the deserted park, the bushes stone,
The snowless grass green shadows under yews,
Each footprint quick and violet as a bruise.

Empty of thought as was the sky of colour,
I saw the dead shoots blur the frozen pallor,
And turned into a narrow path between
The dirt of branches loaded with the clean.

What was it then that pierced my inmost self,
Walking alone along that little gulf:
What archetypal memory of cold,
What wolves, what forests, what unquiet child?

TIME

Stretched in the sun, I see upon my skin
A few and tiny violet veins, like worms—
Not shocked but as the sceptic viewer in
The lenses sees the plasm laced with germs.

The sun turns on, the body's pigmentation
Changes to flame: as gradually, the man
Accommodates the frightening situation,
The unlived years that fold up like a fan.

Time moves through matter at so queer a pace
One seldom sees it truly—sheer and vast.
Only in corners of the human space
Bruises reveal the struggle to hold fast:

Until time's final effort to be free
Involves the whole in stains and agony.

THE IMAGE

A spider in the bath. The image noted:
Significant maybe but surely cryptic.
A creature motionless and rather bloated,
The barriers shining, vertical and white:
Passing concern, and pity mixed with spite.

Next day with some surprise one finds it there.
It seems to have moved an inch or two, perhaps.
It starts to take on that familiar air
Of prisoners for whom time is erratic:
The filthy aunt forgotten in the attic.

Quite obviously it came up through the waste,
Rejects through ignorance or apathy
That passage back. The problem must be faced;
And life go on though strange intruders stir
Among its ordinary furniture.

One jibs at murder, so a sheet of paper
Is slipped beneath the accommodating legs.
The bathroom window shows for the escaper
The lighted lanterns of laburnum hung
In copper beeches—on which scene it's flung.

We certainly would like thus easily
To cast out of the house all suffering things.
But sadness and responsibility
For our own kind lives in the image noted:
A half-loved creature, motionless and bloated.

OWLS

Swaddled in yews as black as ink
The owls sit in a tidy frieze
Like oriental deities,
Unlidding their red eyes. They think.

They will sit on quite motionless
Until that hour, nostalgic, dun,
When, rolling up the slanting sun,
Shadows reoccupy the place.

Their attitude reminds the clever
That in our time and world one never
Ought to seek action, or revolt;

Man shaken by a creeping shade
Bears always in himself the guilt
Of having wished to change his fate.

A DREAM

Unwound the long evolvement,
Mankind was fish again,
Gilled in the fluid prison,
And half absolved from pain.

No rapture and no music,
No agonized despair,
No conscience and no dreaming,
No ecstasies of prayer.

No love to flail the pulses,
Nor love that calms the breast,
But cold mechanic motion,
And cold mechanic rest.

Awake, I cried to heaven,
'God, spin thy spiral fast,
Lest, flinching or lethargic,
Man slides into his past.'

*Mary
Fullerton ('E')*

PASSIVITY

Call not on comfort lest she come
With all her helpers sleek and dumb—
Soft ropes that seem as frail as air,
To bind you in a cushioned chair,
With anodyne, and balm, and spell,
To chant of droning ritual.

Traffic with danger, heat, and strain,
Face when it comes the spear of pain:
None that achieve—the bad, the good—
Have sold to comfort, hardihood.

57

O, flaccid, havened, housed, defended,
Flesh still alive, but *living* ended!
Angels nor devils are of these—
The castaways on velvet ease.

SNOW IN EUROPE

David
Gascoyne

Out of their slumber Europeans spun
Dense dreams: appeasement, miracle, glimpsed flash
Of a new golden era; but could not restrain
The vertical white weight that fell last night
And made their continent a blank.

Hush, says the sameness of the snow
The Ural and the Jura now rejoin
The furthest Arctic's desolation. All is one
Sheer monotone: plain, mountain: country, town:
Contours and boundaries no longer show.

The warring flags hang colourless a while;
Now midnight's icy zero feigns a truce
Between the signs and seasons, and fades out
All shots and cries. But when the great thaw comes,
How red shall be the melting snow, how loud the drums!

SPRING MCMXL

London Bridge is falling down, Rome's burnt, and Babylon
The Great is now but dust; and still Spring must
Swing back through Time's continual arc to earth.
Though every land become as a black field
Dunged with the dead, drenched with the dying's blood,
Still must a punctual goddess waken and ascend
The rocky stairs, up into earth's chilled air,
And pass upon her mission through those carrion ranks,
Picking her way among a maze of broken brick
To quicken with her footsteps the short sooty grass between;
While now once more their futile matchwood empires flare and blaze
And through the smoke men gaze with bloodshot eyes
At the translucent apparition, clad in trembling nascent green,
Of one they can still recognize, though scarcely understand.

THE GIRAFFES

I saw, between a page's turning,
Shapes on the distant desert burning,
Shadows running, swift and far,
Where the white clouds of morning are.

Stella
Gibbons

It was the herds of gold giraffes
That couple with the hippogriffes,
And run with tireless shoulders bare
To the more golden desert air:
The joyous herds that feed on leaves
The sun from hidden rhizomes weaves,
And bathe with great, strong striding flanks
Where hidden waters press their banks:
The herds that sleep not through the night,
But fly through miles of cool blue light,
Circling never nearer than
Seven long leagues in sight of Man:
The gentle herds that die unseen
In Chi's stone vale of age carved green,
And whose delight is still to run
Like wind between the sands and sun.

I hid the thought that suddenly
Troubled my mind's tranquillity.
'What if those golden beasts should find
The secret out before mankind?
And if their draught of movement's wine
Teach them before these books of mine?
If they are nearer to the True
Than Wisdom?' pierced doubt's arrow through.

COVERINGS

I

The snake had shed his brindled skin
To meet the marching feet of spring;
With bar, curve, loop and whirling ring
The patterned swathes, papyrus thin,
Lay on the cage's sanded floor
Marked with dragging python spoor.

Flick-flack! Like ash of vulcanite
His lidless eyes in the spatulate
Head were alive with watchful hate,
Daring the sounds and the raw spring light.
He shone like watered silk from his tongue
To his tapering tail where the skin-shreds hung.

The cloudy yellow of mustard flowers
Was barred on his skin with jetty flares
And the five-patched circle the leopard wears:
The sea-shell's convolute green towers
Were called to mind by his belly's hue
That faded to pallid egg-shell blue.

He was covered so to face the sun:
That shadows of leaves might match his skin;
That, where the lily roots begin,
You might not see where the snake begun;
That Man might see, when Snake was dressed,
God in snake made manifest.

II

Mrs Fand wore a fox round her wrinkled throat;
He was killed at dawn as he snarled his threat
In a bracken-brake where the mist lay wet.
Two men were drowned in a shattered boat
Hunting the whale for the silk-bound shred
That balanced her bust with her henna'd head.

An osprey's plume brushed her fallen chin,
And a lorgnette swung on a platinum chain
To deputize for her sightless brain.
Her high-heeled shoes were of python skin,
Her gloves of the gentle reindeer's hide,
And to make her card-case a lizard died.

She watched the flickering counter-play
As the snake reared up with tongue and eye
Licking the air for newt or fly;
And shook herself as she turned away
With a tolerant movement of her head:
'The nasty, horrid thing!' she said.

LULLABY FOR A BABY TOAD

Sleep, my child:
The dark dock leaf
Spreads a tent
To hide your grief.
The thing you saw
In the forest pool
When you bent to drink
In the evening cool
Was a mask that He,
The Wisest Toad,
Gave us to hide
Our precious load—
The jewel that shines
In the flat toad-head,
With gracious sapphire
And changing red.

For if, my toadling,
Your face were fair
As the precious jewel
That glimmers there,
Man, the jealous,
Man, the cruel,
Would look at you
And suspect the jewel.

So dry the tears
From your hornèd eyes,
And eat your supper
Of dew and flies;
Curl in the shade
Of the nettles deep,
Think of your jewel
And go to sleep.

ANOTHER SPRING

How beautiful the country now   *Douglas*
With blossom white upon the bough,   *Gibson*
As slowly through the ocean sky
The clouds like sailing-ships ride by.

A ploughman goes with steady tread
Across the field, the russet red
Of earth shines golden in the light,
Gashed by the lapwings' black and white.

Though many Springs have come and passed
Each seems more lovely than the last;
But when for me all Springs are done
And darkness shuts out sky and sun . . .

Others will marvel how each year
The miracles of Spring appear,
And with my eyes will find delight
In blossom, sky and lapwings' flight.

AT BROXBOURNE STATION

Our train pulled into the quiet country station,
Sleepy in the sun, English to the bone,
And then I heard an eager chattering
In a strange tongue,
And saw the four coffee-skinned Lascars
In their grey turbans and pale clothes,
And the platform was an Eastern bazaar,
Shot with gesticulation, silks and dust,
Bright carpets, swirl of fabrics unfolding
Through my mind, scents and spices, and the slow
Tolling of bells, blind beggars by the walls
Praying for alms, sun on fabulous jewels;
And the carrier pigeons released by the stolid porter
Flashed rainbow colours over the English scene
On Sultan's palaces and flowering fountains.

THE STRICKEN TREE

Now that the summer once again
Has drenched the trees with emerald fire,
I suddenly can feel the pain
Of this tall leafless stricken spire
Where never bird will build its nest
Nor soft wind through its branches sigh,
Nor join young neighbours dancing, lest
Its limbs should crack, so stiff and dry.

And yet this sun-bleached skeleton
Has a taut beauty of its own:
Its Spring and Summer long since gone
Now stands revealed the shining bone,
The essence of the tree, the truth
Which green-foam beauty hid in youth.

INSENSIBILITY

Death is not in dying,
But the unfeeling
Heart when the winds are crying;
Is a cancer, stealing
Over the bright eyes, glazing
That mirrored plunder,
Once a bright flame, blazing
The world's true wonder.

Death is not in dying,
But in forgoing
Beauty: the white clouds flying,
The swift tides flowing.
That is the real death, leaving
The heart unstirred,
Feeling no pain of grieving,
No singing bird.

THE BLIND-WORM

When I stroked his cold dry skin,
His black tongue flickered out and in.

Flicker your black tongue three times three
If my true love is safe at sea.

I stroked him thrice and thrice, and then
I stroked his cold skin twice again:

And each time out the quick tongue came,
And flickered like a wee black flame.

At three times three, my fingers shook:
I shut my eyes, afraid to look;

And when I opened them the snake
Had vanished in the withered brake.

Wilfrid
Gibson

THE LAST SHIFT

You're surely early home, lad? Your shift's not over?
Ay, my shift is over, lassie, my last shift.
Last shift? You're telling me, you've stopped working!
Ay, I'll never hew again in Hellgut Drift.
Your face is grey and white, lad—your eyes are queer and wild-like:
Something's happened to you on your last shift!
*Something! Ay, lass, I've just slipped home to tell you
I'm straked beneath a ton of coal in Hellgut Drift.*

THE FEATHERS

Stridently cutting through
The diamond flame of heat
That holds the city in a glassy trance,
The searching chanting of the muezzin sings
Above the empty street
From the slim minaret whose lance
Of ivory pierces the dense blue,
Where on still planing wings
A solitary kite,
Dark as charred paper floating in the light,
Hangs hovering; when, as the call to prayer
Sinks to a murmur, suddenly a white
And startled pigeon flutters through the air
In tumbling flight,
And from the glittering height
Death drops on unheard wings;
And as again the dark kite swings
Into the blue, a snowy flutter
Of feathers falls in the deserted square,
And a lean mongrel snoozing in the gutter
Opens one eye and blinks
In the white glare,
Licking warm blood-drops from his muzzle, and sinks
Again in deep
Undreaming sleep:
But the child peering through the latticed shutter
Shivers with sudden cold
To see life stricken in mid-air
And heaven darken with the wings of death,
And instantly grown old

64

Already feels the cruel talons tear
His fluttering heart, and cowers with sobbing breath,
Eyeing with frightened stare
The scatter of white feathers lying there.

A MIDWINTER SCENE

Ready for Christmas, autumn rolls up its sleeves,   *Robert*
Boughs that strip to plunge to the icebare elbow,   *Gittings*
And on the ground the leaves
In black lacquered together.
No rackruin weather

This, but a preparation of climate, a watch
Kept to welcome the rumoured newcoming season,
Whose tinkling footbells catch
The ear one frosty glinting nightfall,
And by morning the rightful

Travellers arrive, the tall white-bearded kings,
Their robes and alpine staffs feathered with snow-flowers,
As each to birthday brings
The world's grey wisdom, orient-keen:—
A midwinter scene.

HIBERNATION

Over the yellow autumn leaves
A late white butterfly slowly glides,
As if it looked, as if it sought for
Summer and something else besides.
But the mists rise on the spider's weaving,
The whistling migrants flock and go,
And half the world's round head is plunging
Into the cap of cold and snow.
Into the blackening glint of frost
The drifting myriads flutter on,
With one last hope, with one last question,
Seeking the sun they know has gone.
The many die; and the few remaining
In rusty barns fold up their wings.
Yet they, whom Spring's green light releases,
Carry the tint of new-born things.

THE HAUNTED HOUSE

Robert
Graves

'Come, surly fellow, come: a song!'
   What, fools? Sing to you?
Choose from the clouded tales of wrong
   And terror I bring to you:

Of a night so torn with cries,
   Honest men sleeping
Start awake with rabid eyes,
   Bone-chilled, flesh creeping,

Of spirits in the web-hung room
   Up above the stable,
Groans, knockings in the gloom,
   The dancing table,

Of demons in the dry well
   That cheep and mutter,
Clanging of an unseen bell,
   Blood choking the gutter,

Of lust filthy past belief
   Lurking unforgotten,
Unrestrainable endless grief
   In breasts long rotten.

A song? What laughter or what song
   Can this house remember?
Do flowers and butterflies belong
   To a blind December?

AN ENGLISH WOOD

This valley wood is pledged
To the set shape of things,
And reasonably hedged:
Here are no harpies fledged,
No rocs may clap their wings,
Nor gryphons wave their stings.
Here, poised in quietude,
Calm elementals brood
On the set shape of things:

They fend away alarms
From this green wood.
Here nothing is that harms—
No bulls with lungs of brass,
No toothed or spiny grass,
No tree whose clutching arms
Drink blood when travellers pass,
No mount of glass;
No bardic tongues unfold
Satires or charms.
Only, the lawns are soft,
The tree-stems, grave and old;
Slow branches sway aloft,
The evening air comes cold,
The sunset scatters gold.
Small grasses toss and bend,
Small pathways idly tend
Towards no fearful end.

THE COOL WEB

Children are dumb to say how hot the day is,
How hot the scent is of the summer rose,
How dreadful the black wastes of evening sky,
How dreadful the tall soldiers drumming by.

But we have speech, to chill the angry day,
And speech, to dull the rose's cruel scent.
We spell away the overhanging night,
We spell away the soldiers and the fright.

There's a cool web of language winds us in,
Retreat from too much joy or too much fear:
We grow sea-green at last and coldly die
In brininess and volubility.

But if we let our tongues lose self-possession,
Throwing off language and its watery clasp
Before our death, instead of when death comes,
Facing the wide glare of the children's day,
Facing the rose, the dark sky and the drums,
We shall go mad no doubt and die that way.

THE PERSIAN VERSION

Truth-loving Persians do not dwell upon
The trivial skirmish fought near Marathon.
As for the Greek theatrical tradition
Which represents that summer's expedition
Not as a mere reconnaissance in force
By three brigades of foot and one of horse
(Their left flank covered by some obsolete
Light craft detached from the main Persian fleet)
But as a grandiose, ill-starred attempt
To conquer Greece—they treat it with contempt;
And only incidentally refute
Major Greek claims, by stressing what repute
The Persian monarch and the Persian nation
Won by this salutary demonstration:
Despite a strong defence and adverse weather
All arms combined magnificently together.

NEW APRIL

Geoffrey
Grigson

The wet and brown-sky'd April mornings,
Speckled by the solid chestnut candles, sluiced
And swollen with songs,
Even more than frost, and shrivelling November,
And decay,
Denote the ludicrous wrongs.

These faces, sweat-grey and emptied in the night,
(Hands clutching at a paper or feet
Shoving a bike along)
Have no will to know the moment or to feel
The petals of the day,
No energy to detain the songs.

The headlines are changing hands for a penny,
Announce death nimbly, and the cut in the heart of metal
Admit no God is either right or wrong—
Grey faces, from an automatic nightmare in the creased
And clammy bed,
We can't declare, it will, or it will not be long.

AUTUMN UNDER THE TREES

Yellow tunnels under trees, long avenues
Long as the whole of time:
A single, aimless man
Carries a black garden broom:
Too far he is to hear him
Wading through the leaves, down autumn
Tunnels, under yellow trees, long avenues.

WHAT ARE THEY THINKING . . .

What are they thinking, the people in churches,   *Bryan*
Closing their eyelids and kneeling to pray,   *Guinness*
Touching their faces and sniffing their fingers,
Folding their knuckles one over another?
What are they thinking? Do they remember
This is the church: and this is the steeple:
Open the door: and here are the people?
Do they still see the parson climbing upstairs,
Opening the window and saying his prayers?
Do they perceive in the pit of their palms
The way of the walls and the spin of the spire,
The turmoil of tombstones tossed in the grass,
Under the yawning billows of yew?
Can they discover, drooping beyond them,
The chestnuts' fountains of flowers and frills,
And the huge fields folded into the hills?

What are they thinking, the sheep on the hills,
Bobbing and bending to nibble the grass,
Kissing the crisp green coat of the combes?
What are they thinking, lying contented
With vacant regard in long rumination?
Do they consider the sky as a cage,
Their fleeces as fetters, their bones as their bonds?
Or do they rejoice at the thyme on their tongues,
The dome of the sky, the slope of the downs,
The village below, the church, and the steeple,
With shepherd and ploughman and parson and people?

And what is he feeling, the lark as he flies,
Does he consider the span of his days,
Does he dissever himself from his spirit,
His flight from his feathers, his song from his singing?

Is he cast down at the thought of his brevity?
Or does he look forward to fond immortality?
He stitches the sky with the thread of his breath
To all the bright pattern of living beneath,
To ploughman and shepherd and parson and people,
To the sheep on the hills and the church and the steeple.

THE WOOD

J. C.
Hall

And once I remember coming through a wood
On a still day, before the flood
Of history broke upon us.
Nothing disturbed me. The onus
Of summer lay lightly on leaves and made
No noise. O walking in the shade
And solitude of that place, the green
Banners, birds, and the magical unseen
Music of insects, seemed
Gathered into my blood, wholly confirmed
And fastened upon my heart.

So now whatever falls apart
In the chaos of these times, the natural tide
Goes on, is free, blossoms and burgeons through the wide
Image of poetry: Wordsworth who fills
The stern mould of all Westmorland hills;
Hardy, too, colossus at the gate,
Between whose limbs men sail in to their fate;
And that most stubborn and age-angry man,
William Yeats, who once with rod and can
Laughed under Ben Bulben's side, but passed
Into a brilliant, bitter song at last.

These names are more than names, their words
More than the words mean. For, lords
Of a landscape, they bequeath
More than a poem to the rolling earth;
Are stones, *are* trees, *are* the first roots that grew
Deeper than spades go. All this I knew
Once in the secret and still room of a wood
And later at the judgment of my blood.

AFTER CHRISTMAS

Gone is that errant star. The shepherds rise
And, packed in buses, go their separate ways
To bench and counter where their flocks will graze
On winter grass, no bonus of sweet hay.
The myrrh, the frankincense fade from memory:
Another year of waiting for the day.

Still in his palace Herod waits for orders:
Arrests, an edict, more judicial murders,
New taxes, reinforcements for the borders.
Still high priests preach decorum, rebels rage
At Caesar battening on their heritage
And a few prophets mourn a godless age.

The Magi in three chauffeur-driven cars
Begin their homeward journey round the wars,
Each to his capital, the stocks and shares
Whose constellations, flickering into place,
Must guide him through a vaster wilderness
Than did the star absconded out of space.

The golden thread winds back upon the spool.
A bird's dry carcass and an empty bottle
Beside the dustbin, vomit of goodwill,
Pale streets, pale faces and a paler sky;
A paper Bethlehem, a rootless tree
Soon to be stripped, dismembered, put away,

Burnt on the grate . . . and dressed in candlelight
When next the shepherds turn their flocks about,
The three wise kings recall their second state
And from the smaller circle of the year,
Axle and weighted hub, look high and far
To pierce their weekday heaven that hides the star.

*Michael
Hamburger*

NEW CITIES

What boast have weeds and grasses, humbling
Brick and lime
Of walls falling and high towers tumbling
To dust, and the dissolution of Time?

*George Rostrevor
Hamilton*

For men, men, forgetting their sorrow,
Build the more,
Bury the past and build for tomorrow,
Strip the plain, and the brown earth score;

Yea, as they pile their white cliff masses
And weld their skeletons of steel rods,
Fling their fathers' towns to the grasses,
Gratis, with the gesture of gods—

And, as the new fierce homes spread over
Tortured earth, till her lap be filled,
Allow the blowing of weeds to cover
The ruins with beauty they cannot build.

HAWK

Things motionless were felt to move
    Downward; the hedges crawled
Down steep sun-molten banks to where
    The shrunken river sprawled:

Dark cloud-ravines of shadow flowed
    Sheer down the dark wood's cliff;
Draped heavily in golden heat,
    The limbs of air fell stiff:

And, threatening doom, the sky's concentrated will
Hung in one black speck, poised above the hill.

BATHYMETER

William
Hart-Smith

Those who have descended to the nethermost deeps
Of the ocean sealed in a bell
Past where the last blue-violet creeps

Imperceptibly away, and have hung
Suspended on a filament in utter dark,
While above them rung on rung

The colours of the spectrum ladder rise,
Say that the fish have lights
Like rows of portholes, dots around their eyes,

Headlamps of fluorescent studs,
Or lanterns hung on poles,
And the darkness is alive with moving buds

Of phosphorescence; fish with dim lit sails,
Shrimps that explode
In an enemy's face, and clouds of luminous snails.

And those who have been up in a balloon
So high the pale blue sky goes dark,
And darker, and the sun and moon

Burn pitilessly, say
The myriad stars appear
Shining at high noon of the brightest day.

In a liquid atmosphere that presses tight
With a multitude of tons,
Fish scrawl an aimless script direct in light;

While high above, a multitude of suns
In eternal night
Dance to a cosmic tune. And midway runs,

Precariously swung between extremes,
Our film of atmosphere, where light's diffused,
A narrow equipoise of pressure, heat and cold. It seems

This dance of stars in solemn time
And fish in swing is certain proof the Lord,
Whoever he be, cannot resist a rhyme.

THE FOX

It was twenty years ago I saw the fox   *Phoebe*
Gliding along the edge of prickling corn,   *Hesketh*
A nefarious shadow
Between the emerald field and bristling hedge,
On velvet feet he went.

Phoebe
Hesketh

The wind was kind, withheld from him my scent
Till my threaded gaze unmasked him standing there,
The colour of last year's beech-leaves, pointed black,
Poised, uncertain, quivering nose aware
Of danger throbbing through each licking leaf.
One foot uplifted, balanced on the brink
Of perennial fear, the hunter hunted stood.

I heard no alien stir in the friendly wood,
But the fox's sculpted attitude was tense
With scenting, listening, with a seventh sense
Flaring to the alert; I heard no sound
Threaten the morning; and followed his amber stare,
But in that hair-breadth moment, that flick of the eye,
He vanished.

And now, whenever I hear the expectant cry
Of hounds on the empty air,
I look to a gap in the hedge and see him there
Filling the space with fear; the trembling leaves
Are frozen in his stillness till I hear
His leashed-up breathing—how the stretch of time
Contracts within the flash of recreation!

BLEASDALE: THE WOODEN CIRCLE

In the sun of a late Summer I return
To the land where I was born—
The true magnetic north with its dark moods
And heather-shouldered fells, where the green corn
Delays the farmers' year.

Here is the stream that washed our youth away
Under the bridge's eye,
And the black unblinking pond, thick-lashed with reeds,
That gazes at but never holds the sky.
And stripped by distance to a line of grey
The naked sea is stretched across the bay.

This country is dynamic, beckoning
Her sons back to the stormy solitudes
And tawny marshes where reluctant Spring
Retards the leaf; vitality unspent
Is leashed within the acorn and the bud.
And in these brooding silences between
Age-twisted oaks and bristled firs, there breathes
A spirit older than the ageless earth.

74

A shawl of sun surrounds the infant church
That of itself can give back merely shadows
From stones that gave it birth.
But the soul of man was born when first he turned
From the dust to gaze in wonder at the sun.
After the seedless silences of cold
He looked to the east and saw his golden god
Risen from nowhere to subdue the night;
And in that hour the unsleeping watch began.

Time falls away; unmeasured ages wheel
Through Ice and Stone and Bronze till now we stand
On the circle where our fathers knew the sun
And knew that it was good.
Here priest and peasant have stood
In the first prayer, facing towards the east.
And wonder, ever young, still gropes behind
The sun for motive, feels the muscled wind
And questions whence it came.
The weather-cock, unresting on the church,
Reflects the mystery of eternal change
Eternally the same.

THE INVADING SPRING

Man has fenced the wilderness back in the hills;
Tamed in the town he walks on concrete blocks;
And in the park his heart with pleasure fills—
But not at Wordsworth's school-book daffodils.
No, his delight is catching up with clocks
And turning knobs and pressing Button A—
The train is due; there's half a minute to go
But the lift's gone down and the escalator's slow—
Praise God for the Underground this lark-song day!

Breathing, yet dead, his life is caged with steel—
Wire, wheel, and cable—automatic aids
To living—he exists but cannot feel
The slow barbaric beauty that invades
A world at Spring. He moves in crowds and queues
And reads the *Morning Star* and the *Evening News*
But cannot read the sky though April beats
A golden fanfare down the dusty streets
And breathes a green breath through the petrol fumes.

Yet a third-floor room is powerless to deny
The feel of leaves, the pollen-smell behind
New flowered cretonnes where a rebel wind
Is strong and blue with ranging through the sky.
And though the files of his mind are entered up
Like office ledgers, unknowing he holds the cup
Brimmed with the light of moons beyond his reach.
The street is thronged with more than he can know—
The Invisibles who know him; without speech
They call him; without form they come and go
And catch him by the sleeve until the slow
Unwilling flesh is beckoned from its task.
Released, he finds the vital stream that spills
A primrose light on sullen window-sills.

IN AUTUMN

And now the robin rubs two stones together
To kindle his autumn song from a single spark;
And through the silent haze this spurt of sound
Flares like a candle-triumph in the dark.

And doldrum leaves, becalmed as grounded birds,
Rise in a whirling flight
To startle sadness with a sudden laughter—
O threaded-with-surprise days follow after
The summer daisy-chain of steadfast growing!

A thin brown hand is throwing
Lassoos across the stubble, the empty meadow,
To catch the last light with long ropes of shadow.
The reaper and the binder stand in silence;
The barns are full; the human storehouse gathered
With memory and nostalgia.
For only man looks back across the river
To where a transient foam of Spring is blowing
Behind the wood-fire-glowing rowan berries.

And now the wind is colder,
Life smoulders round his heart as round a stone;
And he wonders how the realistic robin
Can make a song from pebbles rubbed together.

THE EXPERT

Come with me through the fields this April day—
I see their colours, you their yield of hay.
Idly I watch the black-faced wobbly lambs
While you exactly count them with their dams.
You, the expert, with a measuring eye
Compute the worth of everything you see;
I only know there is no reason why
Sun, rain, and earth combine to make a tree.

You pity me my lack, for while I gaze
On tawny acres where the curlew breed,
Your calculations blind you with the glaze
Of future drain-pipes stacked against the reed.

Now home again, those damson-coloured hills
Are stretched before me, fields and lambs below.
You read the *Evening Post* and cannot know
How the field between us widens as it fills
With pale unprofitable daffodils.

MERLIN

I will consider the outnumbering dead:
For they are the husks of what was rich seed.
Now, should they come together to be fed,
They would outstrip the locusts' covering tide.

Arthur, Elaine, Mordred; they are all gone
Among the raftered galleries of bone.
By the long barrows of Logres they are made one,
And over their city stands the pinnacled corn.

*Geoffrey
Hill*

THE QUICK AND THE DEAD

What shall it profit you and me
To learn the sun's candlepower
Or the speed of light? What are scientists
But human fools when lightning slays a tree
And lays it at their yokel feet: O where
Is the sun's beat in their cold-fingered look?

*Mark
Holloway*

77

In frigid observatories astronomers
Set down the stars and docket every comet
In a book. This spidery symbol
On the fly-walked page is Venus
Caught to earth and laid by a clerk's hand
On this white sheet, colder than death.

Science has shown me, like Mephistopheles
To Faust, pleasures which turn to dust;
It has shown me a robot's world;
Along its railroads of reason I have found
The lust in the dark, the lost hunger
And the ineffective visions of the blind.

While magicians hide the secret of beauty
In a mathematical tag, our hearts
Like wounded birds, failing and falling
Drop to a slow death. Let us find
Our own sun with the naked eye
And spend life's hour on his golden sands;

Let us give Venus up to eternity
That we may know those visions in the sky
As sea knows moon, untutored
And unquestioning. Let us touch time again
Through a thousand purgatorial years
And spin our five senses into the web of stars.

TRAVEL-PIECE

Richard
Hughes

I have seen lightning walking upon the water,
While thunder shook my head like a sieve of corn:
I have felt cold-handed Winter touch me in the dark,
And Atlas-like have borne the burning weighty sun.

I have seen mountains and forests and beautiful cities
Growing empty as a deserted garden:
Mountains, and broken castles: desolate forests,
Where by a hundred paths
The singing Danube giddies through the plain:
I have felt by night its pulse on the boat's shell,
While fishes leapt like hoops in the dim light:
Seen sunrise delicately tread the uneven water.

Then for a while I sat in stranger places,
Dicing with Hunger to pass away the time;
I cut my fingers on the reins of State,
I knew the wicked eye of half-drawn steel
Outstare my own, and reached my hand for help
To my sole comrade, hidden-footed Fear.
So came at length of climb on alien hills,
Where pine trees sang like the fifty-fluted sea,
And Snow let down her hair among the crocuses;
Where I saw men upon that roof of the world
Battle like cats, and utter their terrible notes.

I have walked with the sun shut into my tight head,
And my hands jewelled with flies till my hands bled,
At noon with bared feet in the hot sand;
The span-deep forest sand, where cedars stretch for ever,
And orchids suck weak breath over coloured swamp-water.
Where hot cicadas trill and bright bird never sings
I have seen the glassy wind warp in the hot sun:
The beautiful curved wind where the locusts tread:
Seen leaves of bushes like myriad green eyes,
And big butterflies like heavy voiceless birds.
And in mid-ocean I have seen green tigers
Endlessly burst through pale dense leaves of fog:
Deep in the under-parts of a ship have seen
Men, the innumerable nations of the world
Like lights, dancing: looked in strange fleckt eyes.

I know the prick of turf, the scent of warm trees,
The taste of cheese, the sound of an old clock,
A fire of green ash logs in a stone house,
The lovely cooling touch of driven rain,
The perfect unrepeated shape of the Welsh hills.
—But I have seen smooth familiar things
So thorny grow with criss-cross memories,
It pained to touch them.

Once, when a boy, I saw an old man die
So slowly scarce you knew which way the battle went
Till Pallor came on his cold horse
With certain rumour of defeat:
And the next day I saw men leap from life
Like salmon leap a weir.
At times I have got drunk on brimming eyes;
Wrestled alone with him who comes by night,
And with a drop of scalding oil have lost him:

79

At times, fused night with day in fervent thinking
Till the skull sweated;
Or tumbled with rhythms on a pile of hay
For half a honey-suckled summer.

But all these things I don't mistake for living,
Nor bombast about them for creative writing,
—Romantics, largely spun from my own stomach,
Samples snipped from an enormous fabric:
Though greatly moving me—part of my substance.
Now, coming to manhood, I know I have plunged no deeper
Into thought or doing than a kitten
Trying to dare to pat an electric fan.
And like that kitten, most I do is prompted
By uneasy twitchings in my tail's tip.
Surely it's now high time that something happened,
Something snapped somewhere, and I entered in;
—Ceased to be like the man who painted in the dark,
Then called for a light to see what he had painted?

THE HORSES

Ted
Hughes

I climbed through woods in the hour-before-dawn dark.
Evil air, a frost-making stillness,

Not a leaf, not a bird,—
A world cast in frost. I came out above the wood

Where my breath left tortuous statues in the iron light.
But the valleys were draining the darkness

Till the moorline—blackening dregs of the brightening grey—
Halved the sky ahead. And I saw the horses:

Huge in the dense grey—ten together—
Megalith-still. They breathed, making no move,

With draped manes and tilted hind-hooves,
Making no sound.

I passed: not one snorted or jerked its head.
Grey silent fragments

Of a grey silent world.

I listened in emptiness on the moor-ridge.
The curlew's tear turned its edge on the silence.

Slowly detail leafed from the darkness. Then the sun
Orange, red, red erupted

Silently, and splitting to its core tore and flung cloud,
Shook the gulf open, showed blue,

And the big planets hanging—.
I turned

Stumbling in the fever of a dream, down towards
The dark woods, from the kindling tops,

And came to the horses.
                              There, still they stood,
But now steaming and glistening under the flow of light,

Their draped stone manes, their tilted hind-hooves
Stirring under a thaw while all around them

The frost showed its fires. But still they made no sound.
Not one snorted or stamped,

Their hung heads patient as the horizons,
High over valleys, in the red levelling rays—

In din of the crowded streets, going among the years, the faces,
May I still meet my memory in so lonely a place

Between the streams and the red clouds, hearing curlews,
Hearing the horizons endure.

PIKE

Pike, three inches long, perfect
Pike in all parts, green tigering the gold.
Killers from the egg: the malevolent aged grin.
They dance on the surface among the flies.

Or move, stunned by their own grandeur,
Over a bed of emerald, silhouette
Of submarine delicacy and horror.
A hundred feet long in their world.

In ponds, under the heat-struck lily pads—
Gloom of their stillness:
Logged on last year's black leaves, watching upwards.
Or hung in an amber cavern of weeds

The jaws' hooked clamp and fangs
Not to be changed at this date;
A life subdued to its instrument;
The gills kneading quietly, and the pectorals.

Three we kept behind glass,
Jungled in weed: three inches, four,
And four and a half: fed fry to them—
Suddenly there were two. Finally one

With a sag belly and the grin it was born with.
And indeed they spare nobody.
Two, six pounds each, over two feet long,
High and dry and dead in the willow-herb—

One jammed past its gills down the other's gullet:
The outside eye stared: as a vice locks—
The same iron in this eye
Though its film shrank in death.

A pond I fished, fifty yards across,
Whose lilies and muscular tench
Had outlasted every visible stone
Of the monastery that planted them—

Stilled legendary depth:
It was as deep as England. It held
Pike too immense to stir, so immense and old
That past nightfall I dared not cast

But silently cast and fished
With the hair frozen on my head
For what might move, for what eye might move.
The still splashes on the dark pond,

Owls hushing the floating woods
Frail on my ear against the dream
Darkness beneath night's darkness had freed,
That rose slowly towards me, watching.

SEA-CHRONICLES

Rex
Ingamells

Where old-time ships came, canvas seagull-white,
articulate around our coast, the seas
speak sailors' Spanish, Dutch and Portuguese,
mutter and roar and whisper, day and night.

Lost names are sounded, could we hear aright,
that beat the *Endeavour* by two centuries
inside the Barrier Reef, and mysteries
resolved for which our scholars have no light.

Voices of water tell and tell and tell
the truths we cannot guess, and sun and stars
confirm and store the facts we have not found.

The winds know how a chill foreboding fell
upon a shore, where, jostled in by spars,
lay bodies of the first invaders, drowned.

PRISONERS

Within the wires of the post, unloading the cans of garbage,   *Randall*
The three in soiled blue denim (the white ball on their backs   *Jarrell*
Sending its chilly *North* six yards to the turning blackened
Sights of the cradled rifle, to the eyes of the yawning guard)
Go on all day being punished, go on all month, all year
Loading, unloading; give their child's, beast's sigh—of despair,
Of endurance and of existence, look unexpectingly
At the big guard, dark in his khaki, at the dust of the blazing plain,
At the running or crawling soldiers in their soiled and shapeless green.
The prisoners, the guards, the soldiers—they all, in their way, being
    trained.
From these moments, repeated forever, our own new world will be
    made.

THE METAMORPHOSES

Where I spat in the harbour the oranges were bobbing
All salted and sodden, with eyes in their rinds;
The sky was all black where the coffee was burning,
And the rust of the freighters had reddened the tide.

But soon all the chimneys were burning with contracts,
The tankers rode low in the oil-black bay,
The wharves were a maze of the crated bombers,
And they gave me a job and I worked all day.

And the orders are filled; but I float in the harbour,
All tarry and swollen, with gills in my sides,
The sky is all black where the carrier's burning,
And the blood of the transports is red on the tide.

THE PURSE-SEINE

Robinson
Jeffers

Our sardine fishermen work at night in the dark of the moon; daylight or moonlight
They could not tell where to spread the net, unable to see the phosphorescence of the shoals of fish.
They work northward from Monterey, coasting Santa Cruz; off New Year's Point or off Pigeon Point
The look-out man will see some lakes of milk-colour light on the sea's night-purple; he points, and the helmsman
Turns the dark prow, the motorboat circles the gleaming shoal and drifts out her seine-net. They close the circle
And purse the bottom of the net, then with great labour haul it in.

I cannot tell you
How beautiful the scene is, and a little terrible, then, when the crowded fish
Know they are caught, and wildly beat from one wall to the other of their closing destiny the phosphorescent
Water to a pool of flame, each beautiful slender body sheeted with flame, like a live rocket
A comet's tail wake of clear yellow flame; while outside the narrowing
Floats and cordage of the net great sea-lions come up to watch, sighing in the dark; the vast walls of night
Stand erect to the stars.

Lately I was looking from a night mountain-top
On a wide city, the coloured splendour, galaxies of light: how could I help but recall the seine-net
Gathering the luminous fish? I cannot tell you how beautiful the city appeared, and a little terrible.
I thought, We have geared the machines and locked all together into inter-dependence; we have built the great cities; now
There is no escape. We have gathered vast populations incapable of free survival, insulated
From the strong earth each person in himself helpless, on all dependent. The circle is closed, and the net
Is being hauled in. They hardly feel the cords drawing, yet they shine already. The inevitable mass-disasters
Will not come in our time nor in our children's, but we and our children
Must watch the net draw narrower, government take all powers—or revolution, and the new government
Take more than all, add to kept bodies kept souls—or anarchy, the mass-disasters.

These things are Progress;
Do you marvel our verse is troubled or frowning, while it keeps its
    reason? Or it lets go, lets the mood flow
In the manner of the recent young men into mere hysteria, splintered
    gleams, crackled laughter. But they are quite wrong.
There is no reason for amazement: surely one always knew that
    cultures decay, and life's end is death.

THEIR BEAUTY HAS MORE MEANING

Yesterday morning enormous the moon hung low on the ocean,
Round and yellow-rose in the glow of dawn;
The night-herons flapping home wore dawn on their wings.
    Today
Black is the ocean, black and sulphur the sky,
And white seas leap. I honestly do not know which day is more
    beautiful.
I know that tomorrow or next year or in twenty years
I shall not see these things—and it does not matter, it does not hurt;
They will be here. And when the whole human race
Has been like me rubbed out, they will still be here: storms, moon
    and ocean,
Dawn and the birds. And I say this: their beauty has more meaning
Than the whole human race and the race of birds.

'FIGHTING IN NAKED DESERTS HE THOUGHT
OF HOME'

Fighting in naked deserts he thought of home,   *Sean*
the soldier swallowed by the drouth of war,   *Jennett*
of fields and heavy trees and quiet rivers
and the apple-hearted hollow forests where
the girders of the blackthorn blossomed over
in early spring: and thrushes loved to sing
through all the cool green shadows of the summer
their bell-dropping, water-falling song.

Here earth's bones lie bleached below the sun
and the barrenness of death fills up the eye
all day; and there is never any shelter
from the anger of the sky; nor any sign
of gentleness: grain grinding grain, the dry
sands drag across the days their burning shutter.

I was a labourer in the smoky valley,
within the high wall, the tall dark walls of the mills,
where the hills go up to the wild moor.
I am a dog of the dales, broad is my speech,
and my ways are not the smooth ways of the south,
but hard, and used to keener weather.
All week I worked among the looms
while the cloth slacked out and the shuttles clacked
swiftly, as the woof was shot through the warp
and through my brain dim with the webs of years.
All week I was the servant of the loom,
chained to the steel for the promise of meagre coin,
six days a week, but Sunday comes
soon, and I am my master for the waking day
that found me with my whippet on the moor.
O my faithful lass! Soft was her fell;
her eyes were like deep pools stained with peat,
shafted with light; and intelligent.
She was long in the body, but strong of limb and rib,
and her muscles moved under the skin
like currents in a bay of the river.
She was swift as the wind or as the summer swallow,
and I would pit her with the local dogs,
backing her swiftness with my sweaty coin
and many a shilling have I won with her
to spend on some wet evening in a pub
or buy the tickets at the picture palace
when I took out the girl I meant to marry—
but that is all forgotten with the flesh.
I was a labourer in the smoky valley:
I am a brittle bone projecting from the sand.

WORDS

Geoffrey
Johnson

Let me not fail them, our faithful English words:
The stout plebeian Saxon, homely as herds,
Wholesome as rain, as tangible as tools,
As deadly as pin-pricks to inflated fools,
As fair as moonlight on a face asleep.
With them the Latin, whose patrician sweep

Of purple, to pomp of brazen trumpets blown,
Haunts immemorial aisles of Parian stone.
And those, the Hellenic breed, whose faces wear
The smile of the still Muses carven fair
In a high tower above a city's fever,
Which they outlived and will outlive for ever.

May my affection honour them—and these,
The guttersnipes who have no pedigrees,
Orphans and urchins whom the wastrel sired,
Or whom the clown, in a great moment fired,
Flung on existence as his final joke,
Yet who with radiant faces through the smoke,
Whisper how near and clear the archangels burn;
Who, chirpy-voiced and merry-limbed, can turn
A waste of mud or wilderness of grime
To a gold-shining city not of time.
Oh! not to these would I do any wrong:
They are not least in the bright heaven of song.

THE WOODCARVER

I do not crave the immediate praise of men,
But if it comes, it brings me joy; not gold
Which, as an end considered, might seduce
My single vision, though the man's a fool
To scorn what natural fruits result from toil.

And so you think I carve this forest-frieze
Of cedar for posterity. What is Fame,
Ten thousand years of Fame before the press
And swirl of dusty ages? A footprint clear
And individual, clear a moment longer
Than one before it on unending sand.
And if my fame were deathless, being dead
What should I trouble for the swing from praise
To blame, indifference, and so back again?
It were as idle to aspire to that
As whimper now that millions who were born
And died before I came have never known,
Will never know my work. The mightiest fame
Is local to the calm eternal eye.

So with this pin's head planet where we dwell:
I am known along the Ganges, in Ceylon
A little, in Cochin China not at all,
But were I sung from Greenland to Cape Horn
What rumour of me would reach the Pleiades,
Orion, and the systems wheeling on and on
In silence without end?
                                    No, none is more
Aware than I how foolish I must look
Working along a microscopic groove,
Time infinite before me and behind,
Space infinite around me and above—
A polyp labouring where so many more
Have laboured and will labour. Yet at least
Something will have been fashioned, something left
Shapelier, fairer, finer than it was,
A legacy for men to love, ignore
Or hate, if only for a while.
                                    But most,
I carve this monument because I must,
Because I love it, and because I wish
Before I die to feel the thrill that comes
When what is wrestled with at last leaps clear
To match the vision leaping in the mind.

UNDECEIVED

Except that the orchard boughs are stiff as wire
In a pool of ice, you might believe that the fire
And wind and song of May had loosened petals;
Such ghostly loveliness of moonlight settles
In crooks and gnarls, so beautiful lie the flecks
Of snow in the forks, so anther-fine the specks
Of white on the floor of tunnels between black boles.

It is no flattering fiction that consoles
My heart, no self-deluding dreams of what might be;
But a rooted faith, an undying voice tells me
That hope, the deceiver, cannot deceive for good;
For, soon or late, the stark and bitter rood
On which the world is stretched must truly burst
Into flower and song, and feel no more accurst.

IN HARDWARE STREET

All the bells in Fairyland
Suddenly rang in the mind,
And joy went capering out of hand
With a falling world behind.

Villa on dingy villa broke
In a toppling mist of gold,
Tumults of towers and spires were smoke,
And the rivers of pavement rolled.

Rang all the bells of porcelain
In a world of wild wet green
Beyond the crystal rims of rain;
And I stood, my wits gone clean.

I should have followed, and this my curse is:
The corpse of myself, enclosed
By windows floridly scrolled like hearses,
Feels a lead weight imposed;

The brassy hardness of kerb and rail
Leers in a drizzle of dews,
And the sunlight drowses like fumes of ale
On the beef-red avenues.

ON THE MOUNTAIN

*And if the sufferings of children go to swell the sum of sufferings which was
necessary to pay for truth, then I protest that the truth is not worth such a
price.*—DOSTOIEVSKY.

The bones of the children cried out upon the mountain   *M. K.*
Thin bones, bird bones, crying like birds   *Joseph*
Up the glacier birdfooted tracks
Hens' feet crows' feet, old snow old world.

The blood of the children cried out upon pavements
The burnt flesh of children screamed in the cities.
All over the earth machines stopped
Animals were dumb men stood listening
And this terrible crying accused
    The men in gold braid who make wars
    The men in silk hats who make peace
    The men in leather jackets who make revolutions
    The men in frock coats who break revolutions.

Then from His throne spoke the Lord Jehovah
Saying: bring Me millstones
A mountain of hollow stones for the necks
Of those who offended these My children.
And He was angry, saying: let there be ocean
Unplumbed depths, bewildering fishes
For each transgressor one halter and one stone.
The angry waves roared Aaaahhhhh.

Still the bones of the children cried out
The blood cried from the cobblestones
The paper bones glittering on ice
The honey blood swarming with blue flies.
By the ocean-sea walked the Lord Jehovah
Thinking millenniums; about His feet
Cherubim played ducks and drakes
With the hollow stones. The sea said Hussshhhh.

He heard the feet of a million walking
Unhurried, firm, from valley and plain
Before them ran trembling those to be judged
    Flapping and fumbling
    Mouthing and mumbling
    Stooping and stumbling

Over the icy stones
    The men with gold eyes
    The men with silk hands
    The men with leather hearts
    The men with no faces
To be judged: to be brought to judgement
Before the children's bones, on the holy mountain.

SECULAR LITANY

That we may never lack two Sundays in a week
One to rest and one to play
That we may worship in the liturgical drone
Of the race-commentator and the radio raconteur
That we may avoid distinction and exception
Worship the mean, cultivate the mediocre
Live in a state house, raise forcibly-educated children
Receive family benefits, and standard wages and a pension
And rest in peace in a state crematorium

Saint Allblack
Saint Monday Raceday
Saint Stabilization
   Pray for us.

From all foreigners, with their unintelligible cooking
From the vicious habit of public enjoyment
From kermesse and carnival, high day and festival
From pubs, cafes, bullfights and barbecues
From Virgil and vintages, fountains and fresco-painting
From afterthought and apperception
From tragedy, from comedy
And from the arrow of God
   Saint Anniversaryday
   Saint Arborday
   Saint Labourday
      Defend us.

When the bottles are empty
And the keg runs sour
And the cinema is shut and darkened
And the radio gone up in smoke
And the sports-ground flooded
When the tote goes broke
And the favourite scratches
And the brass bands are silenced
And the car is rusted by the roadside
   Saint Fathersday
   Saint Mothersday
   Saint Happybirthday
      Have mercy on us.

And for your petitioner, poor little Jim,
   Saint Hocus
   Saint Focus
   Saint Bogus
   And Saint Billy Bungstarter
      Have mercy on him.

WILLIAM WORDSWORTH

No room for mourning; he's gone out   *Sidney*
Into the noisy glen, or stands between the stones   *Keyes*
Of the gaunt ridge, or you'll hear his shout
Rolling among the screes, he being a boy again.

91

He'll never fail nor die
And if they laid his bones
In the wet vaults or iron sarcophagi
Of fame, he'd rise at the first summer rain
And stride across the hills to seek
His rest among the broken lands and clouds.
He was a stormy day, a granite peak
Spearing the sky; and look, about its base
Words flower like crocuses in the hanging woods,
Blank though the dalehead and the bony face.

PHEASANT

Cock stubble-searching pheasant, delicate
Stepper, Cathayan bird, you fire
The landscape, as across the hollow lyre
Quick fingers burn the moment: call your mate
From the deep woods tonight, for your surprised
Metallic summons answers me like wire
Thrilling with messages, and I cannot wait
To catch its evening import, half-surmised.
Others may speak these things, but you alone
Fear never noise, make the damp thickets ring
With your assertions, set the afternoon
Alight with coloured pride. Your image glows
At autumn's centre—bright, unquestioning
Exotic bird, haunter of autumn hedgerows.

AGAINST DIVINATION

Not in the night time, in the weary bed
Comes wisdom, neither to the wild
Symbolic leaf of autumn. Never seek
Your solace from the automatic hand
Of medium, or lover's partial gaze:
Truth is not found in book or litten glass
At midnight. Ghosts are liars. None may turn
Winter's hard sentence but the silly man,
The workless plowman or the unhoused poet
Who walks without a thought and finds his peace
In tall clouds mounting the unbroken wind,
In dry leaves beating at the heavens' face.

THE WHITE MOTH

Far into the thundery summer night   *Carla Lanyon*
With up-flung windows wide to the hot garden   *Lanyon*
And, by the open door, one lamp alight,
We talked, a group of friends, young men and women
Who turned the world with talk to set it right,
And all the heavens too, because the burden
Of our argument obliterated God.

A white moth, with wings like a yacht at sea,
Came in out of the dark, spiralled a little,
Lamp drawn, then on the ceiling close to me,
By some strange law of suction, chose to settle,
Four lines on its greater wings joined perfectly
Rigging of lower sails; sensitive, brittle
As stamens were the feet on which it trod.

I saw its furred face, the exact design
Of three black circles set in a triangle,
The pure eurhythmy of all curve and line;
A white moth, antennae just a-tingle,
Poised like a spirit, consummate, divine.
And I forgot our heady talk and wrangle,
Forgot we had obliterated God.

BORN YESTERDAY
for Sally Amis

Tightly-folded bud,   *Philip*
I have wished you something   *Larkin*
None of the others would:
Not the usual stuff
About being beautiful,
Or running off a spring
Of innocence and love—
They will all wish you that,
And should it prove possible,
Well, you're a lucky girl.

But if it shouldn't, then
May you be ordinary;
Have, like other women,
An average of talents:

Not ugly, not good-looking,
Nothing uncustomary
To pull you off your balance,
That, unworkable itself,
Stops all the rest from working.
In fact, may you be dull—
If that is what a skilled,
Vigilant, flexible,
Unemphasized, enthralled
Catching of happiness is called.

SKIN

Obedient daily dress,
You cannot always keep
That unfakable young surface.
You must learn your lines—
Anger, amusement, sleep;
Those few forbidding signs

Of the continuous coarse
Sand-laden wind, time;
You must thicken, work loose
Into an old bag
Carrying a soiled name.
Parch then; be roughened; sag;

And pardon me, that I
Could find, when you were new,
No brash festivity
To wear you at, such as
Clothes are entitled to
Till the fashion changes.

AN ARUNDEL TOMB

Side by side, their faces blurred,
The earl and countess lie in stone,
Their proper habits vaguely shown
As jointed armour, stiffened pleat,
And that faint hint of the absurd—
The little dogs under their feet.

Such plainness of the pre-baroque
Hardly involves the eye until,
It meets his left-hand gauntlet, still
Clasped empty in the other; and
One sees, with a sharp tender shock,
His hand withdrawn, holding her hand.

They would not think to lie so long.
Such faithfulness in effigy
Was just a detail friends would see:
A sculptor's sweet commissioned grace
Thrown off in helping to prolong
The Latin names around the base.

They would not guess how early in
Their supine stationary voyage
The air would change to soundless damage,
Turn the old tenantry away;
How soon succeeding eyes begin
To look, not read. Rigidly they

Persisted, linked, through lengths and breadths
Of time. Snow fell, undated. Light
Each summer thronged the glass. A bright
Litter of birdcalls strewed the same
Bone-riddled ground. And up the paths
The endless altered people came,

Washing at their identity.
Now, helpless in the hollow of
An unarmorial age, a trough
Of smoke in slow suspended skeins
Above their scrap of history,
Only their attitude remains.

Time has transfigured them into
Untruth. The stone fidelity
They hardly meant has come to be
Their final blazon, and to prove
Our almost-instinct almost true:
What will survive of us is love.

BAT

D. H.
Lawrence At evening, sitting on this terrace,
When the sun from the west, beyond Pisa, beyond the mountains of
  Carrara
Departs, and the world is taken by surprise . . .
When the tired flower of Florence is in gloom beneath the glowing
Brown hills surrounding . . .

When under the arches of the Ponte Vecchio
A green light enters against stream, flush from the west,
Against the current of obscure Arno . . .

Look up, and you see things flying
Between the day and the night;
Swallows with spools of dark thread sewing the shadows together.

A circle swoop, and a quick parabola under the bridge arches
Where light pushes through;
A sudden turning upon itself of a thing in the air.
A dip to the water.

And you think:
'The swallows are flying so late!'

Swallows?

Dark air-life looping
Yet missing the pure loop . . .
A twitch, a twitter, an elastic shudder in flight
And serrated wings against the sky,
Like a glove, a black glove thrown up at the light,
And falling back.

Never swallows!
Bats!
The swallows are gone.

At a wavering instant the swallows give way to bats
By the Ponte Vecchio . . .
Changing guard.

Bats, and an uneasy creeping in one's scalp
As the bats swoop overhead!
Flying madly.

Pipistrello!
Black piper on an infinitesimal pipe.
Little lumps that fly in air and have voices indefinite, wildly vindictive;

Wings like bits of umbrella.

Bats!

Creatures that hang themselves up like an old rag, to sleep;
And disgustingly upside down.
Hanging upside down like rows of disgusting old rags
And grinning in their sleep.
Bats!

In China the bat is symbol of happiness.

Not for me!

HUMMING-BIRD

I can imagine, in some otherworld
Primeval-dumb, far back
In that most awful stillness, that only gasped and hummed,
Humming-birds raced down the avenues.

Before anything had a soul,
While life was a heave of Matter, half inanimate,
This little bit chipped off in brilliance
And went whizzing through the slow, vast, succulent stems.

I believe there were no flowers then,
In the world where the humming-bird flashed ahead of creation.
I believe he pierced the slow vegetable veins with his long beak.

Probably he was big
As mosses, and little lizards, they say, were once big.
Probably he was a jabbing, terrifying monster.

We look at him through the wrong end of the long telescope of Time,
Luckily for us.

BAVARIAN GENTIANS

Not every man has gentians in his house
in Soft September, at slow, Sad Michaelmas.

Bavarian gentians, big and dark, only dark
darkening the day-time torch-like with the smoking blueness of
    Pluto's gloom,
ribbed and torch-like, with their blaze of darkness spread blue
down flattening into points, flattened under the sweep of white day
torch-flower of the blue-smoking darkness, Pluto's dark-blue daze,
black lamps from the halls of Dio, burning dark blue,
giving off darkness, blue darkness, as Demeter's pale lamps give off
    light,
lead me then, lead me the way.

Reach me a gentian, give me a torch
let me guide myself with the blue, forked torch of this flower
down the darker and darker stairs, where the blue is darkened on
    blueness;
even where Persephone goes, just now, from the frosted September
to the sightless realm where darkness is awake upon the dark
and Persephone herself is but a voice
or a darkness invisible enfolded in the deeper dark
of the arms Plutonic, and pierced with the passion of dense gloom,
among the splendour of torches of darkness, shedding darkness on the
    lost bride and her groom.

From 'APRIL AND ANGLESEY'

I

Christopher Beeches come late to leaf: branches and boles
Lee embossed, still swing and tower bare
austere in greensoft spring: the massive grey
so faintly green, almost a mere
reflection of impetuous leafy weakness. Yet
high in the blue the fan-splayed branches
hold their strong-folded, arch their moulded buds
of leaf; and then all the others seen
thrusting in all directions, bronzed and rough
like hazel nuts, with the same sheen of light.

Light that lies smooth on shouldered trunks, off-set
by deep sculpted hollows and scored rings,
that dives to a scooped pool of shade
where the great limbs divide, that warms all day
this slow, tremendous and engulfing tree.

II

Bronzing midsummer sun
in April, the pale clay ribbed with ploughing
the hedges spurting leaf and birdsong
the amber bee crawling, the tractor
droning, the lambs strong.

These are not trippers' pleasures:
they go deep, claim possession
and inheritance of earth, from limbs
that have driven the tractor, thrust the share
through stiff soil, from hands
that have delivered lambs.

Always therefore the individual texture
of field's fall, the familiar
unnameable smell of sheep, are remembered
actively by all faculties and members
in this articulated freedom
this inward gesture of belonging.

COCK-PHEASANT

Gilded with leaf-thick paint; a steady
Eye fixed like a ruby rock;
Across the cidrous banks of autumn
Swaggers the stamping pheasant-cock.

The thrusting nut and bursting apple
Accompany his jointed walk,
The creviced pumpkin and the marrow
Bend to his path on melting stalk.

Sure as an Inca priest or devil,
Feathers stroking down the corn,
He blinks the lively dust of daylight,
Blind to the hunter's powder-horn.

Laurie
Lee

For me, alike, this flushed October—
Ripe, and round-fleshed, and bellyful—
Fevers me fast but cannot fright, though
Each dropped leaf shows the winter's skull.

FIELD OF AUTUMN

Slow moves the acid breath of noon
over the copper-coated hill,
slow from the wild crab's bearded breast
the palsied apples fall.

Like coloured smoke the day hangs fire,
taking the village without sound;
the vulture-headed sun lies low
chained to the violet ground.

The horse upon the rocky height
rolls all the valley in his eye,
but dares not raise his foot or move
his shoulder from the fly.

The sheep, snail-backed against the wall,
lifts her blind face but does not know
the cry her blackened tongue gives forth
is the first bleat of snow.

Each bird and stone, each roof and well,
feels the gold foot of autumn pass;
each spider binds with glittering snare
the splintered bones of grass.

Slow moves the hour that sucks our life,
slow drops the late wasp from the pear,
the rose tree's thread of scent draws thin—
and snaps upon the air.

SUNKEN EVENING

The green light floods the city square—
　　A sea of fowl and feathered fish,
　　Where squalls of rainbirds dive and splash
And gusty sparrows chop the air.

Submerged, the prawn-blue pigeons feed
   In sandy grottoes round the Mall,
   And crusted lobster-buses crawl
Among the fountains' silver weed.

There, like a wreck, with mast and bell,
   The torn church settles by the bow,
   While phosphorescent starlings stow
Their mussel shells along the hull.

The oyster-poet, drowned but dry,
   Rolls a black pearl between his bones;
   The typist, trapped by telephones,
Gazes in bubbles at the sky.

Till, with the dark, the shallows run,
   And homeward surges tide and fret—
   The slow night trawls its heavy net
And hauls the clerk to Surbiton.

A BLIND MAN

A blind man in the forest lanes   *John*
Feels with his stick the way to go: *Lehmann*
October's falling sunlight stains
In deeper red the leaves below.

He does not see the squirrel leap
From branch to branch above his head,
The leaf that joins the wrinkled heap
The squirrel's springing feet have shed.

Yet in his shuttered, hueless room
Whose single season has no day,
The images of Autumn come
With scent of nature's moist decay,

And he with quickened thought, divines
The sun-fired alleys miles around,
The beeches in their burning lines,
The drift of embers to the ground.

WAKING FROM SNOW

Beyond the town's black mouth,
The swarming crossroads, the litter of houses,
Spring closes round the rails.

A thousand gardens white with fruit blossom
Wash up to the carriage window,
A wave, an explosion of life
Bursting under the unexpected sun.

And further South, where mountains assemble,
The bathers floating in their lake-canoes
Lie still, like buds just opened.

Earth, waking from snow
Where the train curls down the pass,
Has broken the green fall of the slopes
With an upthrust of crocuses, white and purple.

All the abundance of the chestnut trees,
Their piled flowers among the mountains of leaves,
Remind, will stand as a symbol
Of the explosion of men's lives released from snow
The Spring of hand and heart and mind
That still delays.

INDIA N DAY

I

Alun
Lewis

Dawn's cold imperative compels
Bazaars and gutters to disturb
Famine's casual ugly tableaux.
Lazarus is lifted from the kerb.

The supple sweeper girl goes by
Brushing the dung of camels from the street
The daylight's silver bangles
Glitter on her naked feet.

II

Yellow ramtilla stiffens in the noon,
Jackals skulk among the screes,
In skinny fields the oxen shiver,
The gods have prophesied disease.

Hedges of spike and rubber, hedges of cactus,
Lawns of bougainvilia, jasmine, zinnia,
Terraces of privilege and loathing,
The masterly shadows of a nightmare

Harden and grow lengthy in the drought.
The moneyed antipathetic faces
Converse in courts of pride and fountains
With ermined sleek injustices.
Gods and dacoits haunt the mountains.

III

The sun the thunder and the hunger grow
Extending stupidly the fields of pain
Ploughing the peasant under with his crop
Denying the great mercy of the rain

Denying what each flowering pear and lime
And every child and each embrace imply—
The love that is imprisoned in each heart
By the famines and fortunes of the century.

IV

Night bibles India in her wilderness
The Frontier Mail screams blazing with such terror
The russet tribesman lays aside his flute
Rigid with Time's hypnotic surging error.

The kindness of the heart lies mute
Caught in the impotence of dreams
Yet all night long the boulders sing
The timeless songs of mountain streams.

JIG

C. Day
Lewis

That winter love spoke and we raised no objection, at
Easter 'twas daisies all light and affectionate,
June sent us crazy for natural selection—not
Four traction-engines could tear us apart.
Autumn then coloured the map of our land,
Oaks shuddered and apples came ripe to the hand,
In the gap of the hills we played happily, happily,
Even the moon couldn't tell us apart.

Grave winter drew near and said, 'This will not do at all—
If you continue, I fear you will rue it all.'
So at the New Year we vowed to eschew it
Although we both knew it would break our heart.
But spring made hay of our good resolutions—
Lovers, you may be as wise as Confucians,
Yet once love betrays you he plays you and plays you
Like fishes for ever, so take it to heart.

HORNPIPE

Now the peak of summer's past, the sky is overcast
And the love we swore would last for an age seems deceit:
Paler is the guelder since the day we first beheld her
In blush beside the elder drifting sweet, drifting sweet.

Oh quickly they fade—the sunny esplanade,
Speed-boats, wooden spades, and the dunes where we've lain:
Others will be lying amid the sea-pinks sighing
For love to be undying, and they'll sigh in vain.

It's hurrah for each night we have spent our love so lightly
And never dreamed there might be no more to spend at all.
It's goodbye to every lover who thinks he'll live in clover
All his life, for noon is over soon and night-dews fall.

If I could keep you there with the berries in your hair
And your lacy fingers fair as the may, sweet may,
I'd have no heart to do it, for to stay love is to rue it
And the harder we pursue it, the faster it's away.

WHEN NATURE PLAYS

When nature plays hedge-schoolmaster,
Shakes out the gaudy map of summer
And shows me charabanc, rose, barley-ear
And every bright-winged hummer,

He only would require of me
To be the sponge of natural laws
And learn no more of that cosmography
Than passes through the pores.

Why must I then unleash my brain
To sweat after some revelation
Behind the rose, heedless if truth maintain
On the rose-bloom her station?

When bullying April bruised mine eyes
With sleet-bound appetites and crude
Experiments of green, I still was wise
And kissed the blossoming rod.

Now summer brings what April took,
Riding with fanfares from the south,
And I should be no Solomon to look
My Sheba in the mouth.

Charabancs shout along the lane
And summer gales bay in the wood
No less superbly because I can't explain
What I have understood.

Let logic analyse the hive,
Wisdom's content to have the honey:
So I'll go bite the crust of things and thrive
While hedgerows still are sunny.

BUT TWO THERE ARE . . .

But Two there are, shadow us everywhere
And will not let us be till we are dead,
Hardening the bones, keeping the spirit spare,
Original in water, earth and air,
Our bitter cordial, our daily bread.

C. Day
Lewis

Turning over old follies in ante-room,
For first-born waiting or for late reprieve,
Watching the safety-valve, the slackening loom,
Abed, abroad, at every turn and tomb
A shadow starts, a hand is on your sleeve.

O you, my comrade, now or tomorrow flayed
Alive, crazed by the nibbling nerve; my friend
Whom hate has cornered or whom love betrayed,
By hunger sapped, trapped by a stealthy tide,
Brave for so long but whimpering in the end:

Such are the temporal princes, fear and pain,
Whose borders march with the ice-fields of death,
And from that servitude escape there's none
Till in the grave we set up house alone
And buy our liberty with our last breath.

TWO SONGS

I've heard them lilting at loom and belting,
Lasses lilting before dawn of day:
But now they are silent, not gamesome and gallant—
The flowers of the town are rotting away.

There was laughter and loving in the lanes at evening;
Handsome were the boys then, and girls were gay.
But lost in Flanders by medalled commanders
The lads of the village are vanished away.

Cursed be the promise that takes our men from us—
All will be champion if you choose to obey:
They fight against hunger but still it is stronger—
The prime of our land grows cold as the clay.

The women are weary, once lilted so merry,
Waiting to marry for a year and a day;
From wooing and winning, from owning or earning
The flowers of the town are all turned away.

Come, live with me and be my love,
And we will all the pleasures prove
Of peace and plenty, bed and board,
That chance employment may afford.

I'll handle dainties on the docks
And thou shalt read of summer frocks:
At evening by the sour canals
We'll hope to hear some madrigals.

Care on thy maiden brow shall put
A wreath of wrinkles, and thy foot
Be shod with pain: not silken dress
But toil shall tire thy loveliness.

Hunger shall make thy modest zone
And cheat fond death of all but bone—
If these delights thy mind may move,
Then live with me and be my love.

THE ECSTATIC

Lark, skylark, spilling your rubbed and round
Pebbles of sound in air's still lake,
Whose widening circles fill the noon; yet none
Is known so small beside the sun:

Be strong your fervent soaring, your skyward air!
Tremble there, a nerve of song!
Float up there where voice and wing are one,
A singing star, a note of light!

Buoyed, embayed in heaven's noon-wide reaches—
For soon light's tide will turn—Oh stay!
Cease not till day streams to the west, then down
That estuary drop down to peace.

WILL IT BE SO AGAIN?

Will it be so again
That the brave, the gifted are lost from view,
And empty, scheming men
Are left in peace their lunatic age to renew?
Will it be so again?

Must it be always so
That the best are chosen to fall and sleep
Like seeds, and we too slow
In claiming the earth they quicken, and the old usurpers reap
What they could not sow?

Will it be so again—
The jungle code and the hypocrite gesture?
A poppy wreath for the slain
And a cut-throat world for the living? that stale imposture
Played on us once again?

Will it be as before—
Peace, with no heart or mind to ensure it,
Guttering down to war
Like a libertine to his grave? We should not be surprised:
    we knew it
Happen before.

Shall it be so again?
Call not upon the glorious dead
To be your witnesses then.
The living alone can nail to their promise the ones who said
It shall not be so again.

OF MOURNERS

Dorothy
Livesay

Mourn not for man, speeding to lay waste
The essence of a countryside's most chaste
And ageless contour; her cool-breasted hills,
Purled streams, bare choirs in wood, fair daffodils—

Mourn not, as maudlin singers did, the scars
Left by the slag, industrial wars,
Men tearing fields apart for railway towns
Wresting the silly sheep from sleepy downs:

And sing no more the sentimental song
Of spinning jenny holding lads too long,
Of children toiling underground, or laws
For hanging witches, burning corn for cause.

Sing only with gibing Chaucer's tongue
Of foible and grave fault; of words unsung,
More pungent victory than battles won:
Sing deeds neglected, desecrations done

Not on the lovely body of the world
But on man's building heart, his shaping soul.
Mourn, with me, the intolerant, hater of sun:
Child's mind maimed before he learns to run.

SUMMER FARM

Straws like tame lightnings lie about the grass   *Norman*
And hang zigzag on hedges. Green as glass   *MacCaig*
The water in the horse-trough shines.
Nine ducks go wobbling by in two straight lines.

A hen stares at nothing with one eye,
Then picks it up. Out of an empty sky
A swallow falls and, flickering through
The barn, dives up again into the dizzy blue.

I lie, not thinking, in the cool, soft grass,
Afraid of where a thought might take me—as
This grasshopper with plated face
Unfolds his legs and finds himself in space.

Self under self, a pile of selves I stand
Threaded on time, and with metaphysic hand
Lift the farm like a lid and see
Farm within farm, and in the centre, me.

JUVENILE DELINQUENCY

Who threw the stone that brought the window down   *Donagh*
What hand was glutted in the toffee jar   *MacDonagh*
Who slipped behind the counter for half-a-crown
What dusty finger blasphemed on the motor-car

And who Oh who was hurried from the class-room
Who was a barbed Saint Stephen feathered with guilt
Who took a hammer to the family heirloom
Who broke who tore who shattered and who spilt

Whose is the dirty face that snivels reform
Who promises a future bright safe whole and new
Who learns at last to wear the uniform
That masks the criminal record from the view?

A WARNING TO CONQUERORS

This is the country of the Norman tower,
The graceless keep, the bleak and slotted eye
Where fear drove comfort out; straw on the floor
Was price of conquering security.

They came and won, and then for centuries
Stood to their arms; the face grew bleak and lengthened
In the night vigil, while their foes at ease
Sang of the strangers and the towers they strengthened.

Ragweed and thistle hold the Norman field
And cows the hall where Gaelic never rang
Melodiously to harp or spinning-wheel.
Their songs are spent now with the voice that sang;

And lost their conquest. This soft land quietly
Engulfed them like the Saxon and the Dane—
But kept the jutted brow, the slitted eye;
Only the faces and the names remain.

VISIT TO ROUEN

Louis
MacNeice

Where she was burned the early market
Deploys its batteries of green;
Only the carrots mimic flame
And all the voices are without.

In hairdressers' and drapers' windows
They drape and crimp five hundred years
Of what was not concerned with dress,
Of what was of the earth, devout.

Westward the cranes look down their noses
Like seahorses, the steamers cry
Between green hills, eastward the bombs
Have made the cathedral graft a skin.

So, between glamour and big business,
Picture postcards and brass tacks,
This town exists upon the surface—
Yet such a surface can wear thin.

And show us gulfs of joy and horror
And bring a name to life, remind
Trader and tripper, bell and siren,
That Joan heard voices from within.

JIGSAWS

II

Property! Property! Let us extend
Soul and body without end:
A box to live in, with airs and graces,
A box on wheels that shows its paces,
A box that talks or that makes faces,
And curtains and fences as good as the neighbours'
To keep out the neighbours and keep us immured
Enjoying the cold canned fruit of our labours
In a sterilized cell, unshared, insured.

Property! Property! When will it end?
When will the Poltergeist ascend
Out of the sewer with chopper and squib
To burn the mink and the baby's bib
And cut the tattling wire to town
And smash all the plastics, clowning and clouting,
And stop all the boxes shouting and pouting
And wreck the house from the aerial down
And give these ingrown souls an outing?

Louis
MacNeice

The gulf between us and the brutes,
Though deep, seems not too wide. Their games,
Though played with neither bats nor boots,
Though played with neither rules nor names,
Seem motivated much as ours—
Not mentioning hungers lusts and fears.

Cow flicking tail, cat sharpening claws,
Dolphin a-gambol, bird a-wheel—
Transpose our hands to fins, to paws,
To wings, we more or less can feel
The same as they; the intellect
Is all we add to it, or subtract.

The iceberg of our human lives
Being but marginal in air,
Our lonely eminence derives
From the submerged nine-tenths we share
With all the rest who also run,
Shuddering through the shuddering main.

PRAYER BEFORE BIRTH

I am not yet born; O hear me.
Let not the bloodsucking bat or the rat or the stoat or the
    club-footed ghoul come near me.

I am not yet born; console me.
I fear that the human race may with tall walls wall me,
    with strong drugs dope me, with wise lies lure me,
        on black racks rack me, in blood-baths roll me.

I am not yet born; provide me
With water to dandle me, grass to grow for me, trees to talk
    to me, sky to sing to me, birds and a white light
        in the back of my mind to guide me.

I am not yet born; forgive me
For the sins that in me the world shall commit, my words
    when they speak me, my thoughts when they think me,
      my treason engendered by traitors beyond me,
        my life when they murder by means of my
          hands, my death when they live me.

I am not yet born; rehearse me
In the parts I must play and the cues I must take when
    old men lecture me, bureaucrats hector me, mountains
    frown at me, lovers laugh at me, the white
      waves call me to folly and the desert calls
        me to doom and the beggar refuses
          my gift and my children curse me.

I am not yet born; O hear me,
Let not the man who is beast or who thinks he is God
    come near me.

I am not yet born; O fill me
With strength against those who would freeze my
    humanity, would dragoon me into a lethal automaton,
      would make me a cog in a machine, a thing with
        one face, a thing, and against all those
        who would dissipate my entirety, would
          blow me like thistledown hither and
            thither or hither and thither
            like water held in the
              hands would spill me.

Let them not make me a stone and let them not spill me.
Otherwise kill me.

MORNING SUN

Shuttles of trains going north, going south, drawing threads of blue,
The shining of the lines of trams like swords,
Thousands of posters asserting a monopoly of the good, the beautiful,
    the true,
Crowds of people all in the vocative, you and you,
The haze of the morning shot with words.

Yellow sun comes white off the wet streets but bright
Chromium yellows in the gay sun's light,
Filleted sun streaks the purple mist,
Everything is kissed and reticulated with sun
Scooped up and cupped in the open fronts of shops
And bouncing on the traffic which never stops.

And the street fountain blown across the square
Rainbow trellises the air and sunlight blazons
The red butcher's and scrolls of fish on marble slabs,
Whistled bars of music crossing silver sprays
And horns of cars, touché, touché, rapiers' retort, a moving cage,
A turning page of shine and sound, the day's maze.

But when the sun goes out, the streets go cold, the hanging meat
And tiers of fish are colourless and merely dead,
And the hoots of cars neurotically repeat and the tiptoed feet
Of women hurry and falter whose faces are dead;
And I see in the air but not belonging there
The blown grey powder of the fountain grey as the ash
That forming on a cigarette covers the red.

SUNDAY MORNING

Down the road someone is practising scales,
The notes like little fishes vanish with a wink of tails,
Man's heart expands to tinker with his car
For this is Sunday morning, Fate's great bazaar;
Regard these means as ends, concentrate on this Now,
And you may grow to music or drive beyond Hindhead anyhow,
Take corners on two wheels until you go so fast
That you can clutch a fringe or two of the windy past,
That you can abstract this day and make it to the week of time
A small eternity, a sonnet self contained in rhyme.

But listen, up the road, something gulps, the church spire
Opens its eight bells out, skull's mouths which will not tire
To tell how there is no music or movement which secures
Escape from the weekday time. Which deadens and endures.

POSTED

Dream after dream I see the wrecks that lie   *John*
Unknown of man, unmarked upon the charts,   *Masefield*
Known of the flat-fish with the withered eye,
And seen by women in their aching hearts.

World-wide the scattering is of those fair ships
That trod the billow tops till out of sight:
The cuttle mumbles them with horny lips,
The shells of the sea-insects crust them white.

In silence and in dimness and in greenness
Among the indistinct and leathery leaves
Of fruitless life they lie among the cleanness.
Fish glide and flit, slow under-movement heaves:

But no sound penetrates, not even the lunge
Of live ships passing, nor the gannet's plunge.

AFTER DEATH

And there will be just as rich fruits to cull   *R. A. K.*
   and jewels to see   *Mason*
   nor shall the moon nor the sun be any more dull
   and there will be flowers as fine to pull
   and the rain will be as beautiful
   but not for me

And there shall be no splendour gone from the vine
   nor from the tree
   and still in the heavens shall glow Jah's radiant sign
   and the dancing sun on horses' sleek hides shall seem no less fine
   still shall the car sweep along with as lovely a line
   but not for me

And men shall cut no less curious things upon brass
   still sweep the sea
   nor no little lustrous shadow upon the sand's mass
   cast by the lilting ripple above shall cease to pass
   and radiance still shall enhalo shadows on moonlit grass
   but not for me.

Huw
Menai

Miraculous alchemy! The hills appear
As if they'd suddenly been greyed by shock,
    Or drenched by spume of stars
    In some celestial storm.

Rimed is the spray to which the robin clings,
That loyal, valiant Knight of the burning shield,
    Who, riding astride a song,
    Gives battle to despair!

Hoar-tinselled poplars stand like morning ghosts,
And spikes of ice frill now the ivy leaf,
    And silver lamps festoon
    The swaying spider's web.

Caught in the larger net spun by the stars
All things are now—stone, grass, wild scrub and tree—
    Snared by a gemmed surprise
    Whose chill no pity knows.

Which stems the flowing sap, corrodes and kills
All unsuspecting fragile tenderness,
    But toughens what survives
    For fuller, stouter growth!

THREE SONNETS

I

Edna St Vincent
Millay

Tranquillity at length, when autumn comes,
Will lie upon the spirit like that haze
Touching far islands on fine autumn days
With tenderest blue, like bloom on purple plums;
Harvest will ring, but not as summer hums,
With noisy enterprise—to broaden, raise,
Proceed, proclaim, establish: autumn stays
The marching year one moment; stills the drums.
Then sits the insistent cricket in the grass;
But on the gravel crawls the chilly bee;
And all is over that could come to pass
Last year; excepting this: the mind is free
One moment, to compute, refute, amass,
Catalogue, question, contemplate, and see.

And if I die, because that part of me
Which part alone of me had chance to live,
Chose to be honour's threshing-floor, a sieve
Where right through wrong might make its ways, and be;
If from all taint of indignation, free
Must be my art, and thereby fugitive
From all that threatens it—why—let me give
To moles my dubious immortality.
For, should I cancel by one passionate screed
All that in chaste reflection I have writ,
So that again not ever in bright need
A man shall want my verse and reach for it,
I and my verses will be dead indeed,—
That which we died to champion, hurt no whit.

3

Read history: so learn your place in Time;
And go to sleep: all this was done before;
We do it better, fouling every shore;
We disinfect, we do not probe, the crime.
Our engines plunge into the seas, they climb
Above our atmosphere: we grow not more
Profound as we approach the ocean's floor;
Our flight is lofty, it is not sublime.
Yet long ago this Earth by struggling men
Was scuffed, was scraped by mouths that bubbled mud;
And will be so again, and yet again;
Until we trace our poison to its bud
And root, and there uproot it: until then,
Earth will be warmed each winter by man's blood.

From THE NORMAN CHURCH

Between the woods in folded lands
An accidental village stands,
Untidily, and with an air
Of wondering who left it there.
Four-square upon a little hill
The Norman Church is Norman still;
And on the winding road below
The ageing houses come and go,
Grey-faced and wrinkled, in a long indented row.

A. A.
Milne

High on the Norman tower the clock
Has kept its faith beneath the shock
Of alien bombs, and, wet or fine,
Maintains that it is ten to nine.
The Vicar used to look and sigh
To think the very Church could lie;
And daily went upon his knees
Petitioning that it might please
Or God or some small clerk to grant priorities.

Meanwhile on Sundays, prim, sedate,
Parishioners would congregate—
By proxies, mostly, found among
The women and the very young;
With, here and there, an elder who
Had either little else to do,
Or, nearing ninety, deemed it well
(Because, of course, you couldn't tell)
To take insurance out, in case there *was* a Hell.

Not all were such; for one could find
A few of undivided mind,
For whom the service of the Lord
Was equal duty and reward.
They followed as established truth
The Faith which they had learnt in youth;
And knowing, without knowing why,
That God the Father reigned on high,
Came there to worship him in all sincerity.

The service winds its placid way:
The Creed, the Collect of the Day,
The Lessons, the appointed Psalms,
The Hymns (with interval for alms);
The Prayer for Rain, if rain be lacked;
If sun, a Prayer for Sun: in fact,
A nicely regulated flow
Of all we want on earth below—
(In places where they *ski*, no doubt a Prayer for Snow).

SUBURBAN DREAM

Edwin
Muir

Walking the suburbs in the afternoon
In summer when the idle doors stand open
  And the air flows through the rooms
  Fanning the curtain hems,

118

You wander through a cool elysium
Of women, schoolgirls, children, garden talks,
      With a schoolboy here and there
      Conning his history book.

The men are all away in offices,
Committee-rooms, laboratories, banks,
      Or pushing cotton goods
      In Wick or Ilfracombe.

The massed unanimous absence liberates
The light keys of the piano and sets free
      Chopin and everlasting youth,
      Now, with the masters gone.

And all things turn to images of peace,
The boy curled over his book, the young girl poised
      On the path as if beguiled
      By the silence of a wood.

It is a child's dream of a grown-up world.
But soon the brazen evening clocks will bring
      The tramp of feet and brisk
      Fanfare of motor horns
      And the masters come.

HORESS

Those lumbering horses in the steady plough,
On the bare field—I wonder why, just now,
They seemed terrible, so wild and strange,
Like magic power on the stony grange.

Perhaps some childish hour has come again,
When I watched fearful, through the blackening rain,
Their hooves like pistons in an ancient mill
Move up and down, yet seem as standing still.

Their conquering hooves which trod the stubble down
Were ritual that turned the field to brown,
And their great hulks were seraphim of gold,
Or mute ecstatic monsters on the mould.

And oh the rapture, when, one furrow done,
They marched broad-breasted to the sinking sun!
The light flowed off their bossy sides in flakes;
The furrows rolled behind like struggling snakes.

But when at dusk with steaming nostrils home
They came, they seemed gigantic in the gloam,
And warm and glowing with mysterious fire
That lit their smouldering bodies in the mire.

Their eyes as brilliant and as wide as night
Gleamed with a cruel apocalyptic light.
Their manes the leaping ire of the wind
Lifted with rage invisible and blind.

Ah, now it fades! it fades! and I must pine
Again for that dread country crystalline,
Where the blank field and the still-standing tree
Were bright and fearful presences to me.

SCOTLAND'S WINTER

Now the ice lays its smooth claws on the sill,
The sun looks from the hill
Helmed in his winter casket,
And sweeps his arctic sword across the sky.
The water at the mill
Sounds more hoarse and dull.
The miller's daughter walking by
With frozen fingers soldered to her basket
Seems to be knocking
Upon a hundred leagues of floor
With her light heels, and mocking
Percy and Douglas dead,
And Bruce on his burial bed,
Where he lies white as may
With wars and leprosy,
And all the kings before
This land was kingless,
And all the singers before
This land was songless,
This land that with its dead and living waits the Judgment Day.

But they, the powerless dead,
Listening can hear no more
Than a hard tapping on the sounding floor
A little overhead
Of common heels that do not know
Whence they come or where they go
And are content
With their poor frozen life and shallow banishment.

SOUTH CUMBERLAND, 10 May 1943

The fat flakes fall
In parachute invasion from the yellow sky.
The streets are quiet and surprised; the snow
Clutters the roofs with a wet crust, but no
Dry harbour is found on soil or wall.

Norman
Nicholson

In the town
The fledgling sparrows are puzzled and take fright;
The weedy hair of the slagbank in an hour turns white.
Flakes fill the tulips in backyard plots;
The chimneys snow upward and the snow smokes down.

Beyond the fells
Dawn lumbers up, and the peaks are white through the mist.
The young bracken is buttoned with snow; the knobs
Of crabapple trees are in bloom again, and blobs
Hang on the nettles like canterbury bells.

The job is mine
And everyone's: to force our blood into the bitter day.
The hawthorn scorched and blasted by the flames of the wind
On the sheltered side greens out a dogged spray—
And this is our example, our duty and our sign.

MICHAELMAS

Like a hound with nose to the trail
The 'bus follows the road;
The road leaps up the hill.
In the valley the railway line is carved like a groove in wood;
The little towns smoke in the hollows;
The slagbanks are grey beneath the brown, bludgeoning fell.

Norman
Nicholson This is the day the air has eyes,
And the Devil falls like hail
From the bright and thundering skies,
And soaks into soil and rock,
And the bad blood rises in nettle and dock,
And toadstools burst like boils between the toes of the trees.

The war that began in heaven still goes on.
Thorn trees twist like spears,
The owl haunts the grain,
The coursed rabbit weeps icicles of tears;
But the feathers of the clouds foretell
St Michael's victory in the purged and praising rain.

SHORTEST DAY, 1942
For N.W.

The damp December light
Settles like fog on roofs
And gable-ends of slate;
The wind blows holes in the sky; the rain
Shines on the road like tin,
And rain-drops hang on the privet, round and white.

Behind a freestone wall,
Between the houses and the street,
In twelve or less square feet
Of tarmac and black soil
Blooms the purple primula
Bright as a lollipop or an aniseed ball.

And so a smile will flower,
A kiss like a child's laugh, or more
Like a friendly terrier's bark,
While the town huddles beneath a dark
Drizzle of misery, and the wind
Flings down sleet from the frozen fells of war.

CLEATOR MOOR

From one shaft at Cleator Moor
They mined for coal and iron ore.
This harvest below ground could show
Black and red currants on one tree.

In furnaces they burnt the coal,
The ore was smelted into steel,
And railway lines from end to end
Corseted the bulging land.

Pylons sprouted on the fells,
Stakes were driven in like nails,
And the ploughed fields of Devonshire
Were sliced with the steel of Cleator Moor.

The land waxed fat and greedy too,
It would not share the fruits it grew,
And coal and ore, as sloe and plum,
Lay black and red for jamming time.

The pylons rusted on the fells,
The gutters leaked beside the walls,
And women searched the ebb-tide tracks
For knobs of coal or broken sticks.

But now the pits are wick with men,
Digging like dogs dig for a bone:
For food and life *we* dig the earth—
In Cleator Moor they dig for death.

Every waggon of cold coal
Is fire to drive a turbine wheel:
Every knuckle of soft ore
A bullet in a soldier's ear.

The miner at the rockface stands,
With his segged and bleeding hands
Heaps on his head the fiery coal,
And feels the iron in his soul.

ST LUKE'S SUMMER

The low sun leans across the slanting field,
And every blade of grass is striped with shine
And casts its shadow on the blade behind,
And dandelion clocks are held
Like small balloons of light above the ground.

Beside the trellis of the bowling green
The poppy shakes its pepper-box of seed;
Groundsel feathers flutter down;
Roses exhausted by the thrust of summer
Lose grip and fall; the wire is twined with weed.

The soul, too, has its brown October days—
The fancy run to seed and dry as stone,
Rags and wisps of words blown through the mind;
And yet while dead leaves clog the eyes
Never-predicted poetry is sown.

THE BLACKBERRY

Between the railway and the mine,
Brambles are in fruit again.
    Their little nigger fists they clench,
    And hold the branches in a clinch.
Waggons of ore are shunted past,
And spray the berries with red dust,
    Which dulls the bright mahogany
    Like purple sawdust clogged and dry.
But when the housewife, wind-and-rain,
Rubs the berry spick and span,
    Compound it gleams like a fly's eye,
    And every ball reflects the sky.
There the world's repeated like
Coupons in a ration book;
    There the tall curved chimneys spread
    Purple smoke on purple cloud.
Grant us to know that hours rushed by
Are photographed upon God's eye;
    That life and leaf are both preserved
    In gelatine of Jesus' blood.
And grant to us the sense to feel
The large condensed within the small;
    Wash clear our eyes that we may see
    The sky within the blackberry.

THE BEACHCOMBER

W. H.
Oliver

Tall ships were wrecked here, and exotic cargoes
Spilled on the beach, not yet for the wave
And rock to disfigure, for the inquisitive gull to discard,

124

But for his delectation; for the space of an hour
Between tide and conquering tide
He could walk among an old world's refuse,
Decking worn smooth and bone fretted on rock,
Metal turned golden and red and shaped like small roses,
Run his fingers through them, until the whorled shell,
The ocean's own grace, became part of his own fancy;
And then walk homewards as the tide gathered,
With his head full of ghosts.
And the wild wave carried
Shells, bone and roses, into a common fortune
And walking homewards, he knew that the time was soon coming
When the wave would gather him also
And his white bones mingle
With that old imaginable world
Of roses hammered from gold and dyed with his own blood.

CALL NOT TO ME

Call not to me when summer shines,   *Ruth*
Death, for in summer I will not go;   *Pitter*
When the tall grass falls in whispering lines
Call not loud from the shades below;
While under the willow the waters flow,
While willow waxes and waters wane,
When wind is slumbrous and water slow,
And woodbine waves in the wandering lane,
Call me not, for you call in vain,
Vain in the time when flowers blow.

But I will hear you when all is bare;
Call and welcome when leaves lie low;
When the dry bents hiss in the raving air
And shepherds from eastward smell the snow;
When the mead is left for the wind to mow,
And the storm is woodman to all the sere,
When hail is the seed the heavens sow,
When all is deadly and naught is dear—
Call and welcome, for I shall hear,
I shall be ready to rise and go.

THE LOST HERMITAGE

Templo valedixi cum osculo . . . SAMUEL JOHNSON

Ruth
Pitter

I'll none of Time:
I leave this place? this roof come down?
This is a graveyard jest, a dream
Too hard for rhyme:
We'll laugh at it when we sit down
Before God's Christmas fire, and tell
Our tales of worms, and ghosts, and hell,
That our eternal hearth securer seem.

My heart dwells here,
In rotten hut on weeping clay;
Tends here her useful herbs, her bloom;
Will not away,
May not be startled to one tear,
Is tenant of her little room
For ever, though they raze
Her cell, and rear a prison in its place.

Stockdove in oak,
Stormcock in elder, finch in thorn,
The blackbird in the quicken, jay,
Starling that spoke
Under the roof before the day,
Titmouse abhorred when damsons bud
And song-thrush hatched in cup of mud:

Frost on the grass,
The lonely morning, the still kine,
Grief for the quick, love for the dead;
The little hill's unchanging line
And nightingale so near my bed,
Pass and return, return and pass,
This time like many a time that was,
Many to be,
Swelling and lapsing seasons lulling me:

All these are laid
Safe up in me, and I will keep
My dwelling thus though it be gone:
My store is not in gold, but made
Of toil and sleep

And wonder walking all alone;
So time's brought low,
My heart's above all he can bring,
And forth in spite of him will go
To gather acorns: ay and sing.

THE BAT

Lightless, unholy, eldritch thing,
Whose murky and erratic wing
Swoops so sickenly, and whose
Aspect to the female Muse
Is a demon's, made of stuff
Like tattered, sooty waterproof,
Looking dirty, clammy, cold.

Wicked, poisonous, and old;
I have maligned thee! . . . for the Cat
Lately caught a little bat,
Seized it softly, bore it in.
On the carpet, dark as sin
In the lamplight, painfully
It limped about, and could not fly.

Even fear must yield to love,
And pity makes the depths to move.
Though sick with horror, I must stoop,
Grasp it gently, take it up,
And carry it, and place it where
It could resume the twilight air.

Strange revelations! warm as milk,
Clean as a flower, smooth as silk!
O what a piteous face appears,
What great fine thin translucent ears!
What chestnut down and crapy wings,
Finer than any lady's things—
And O a little one that clings!

Warm, clean, and lovely, though not fair,
And burdened with a mother's care;
Go hunt the hurtful fly, and bear
My blessing to your kind in air.

127

THE VIPER

Barefoot I went and made no sound;
The earth was hot beneath:
The air was quivering around,
The circling kestrel eyed the ground
And hung above the heath.

There in the pathway stretched along
The lovely serpent lay:
She reared not up the heath among,
She bowed her head, she sheathed her tongue,
And shining stole away.

Fair was the brave embroidered dress,
Fairer the gold eyes shone:
Loving her not, yet did I bless
The fallen angel's comeliness;
And gazed when she had gone.

THE PARADOX

Our death implicit in our birth,
We cease, or cannot be;
And know when we are laid in earth
We perish utterly.

And equally the spirit knows
The indomitable sense
Of immortality, which goes
Against all evidence.

See faith alone, whose hand unlocks
All mystery at a touch
Embrace the awful Paradox
Nor wonder overmuch.

NAMAQUALAND AFTER RAIN

William
Plomer

Again the veld revives,
Imbued with lyric rains,
And sap re-sweetening dry stalks
Perfumes the quickening plains;

Small roots explode in strings of stars,
Each bulb gives up its dream,
Honey drips from orchid throats,
Jewels each raceme;

The desert sighs at dawn—
As in another hemisphere
The temple lotus breaks her buds
On the attentive air—

A frou-frou of new flowers,
Puff of unruffling petals,
While rods of sunlight strike pure streams
From rocks beveined with metals;

Far in the gaunt karroo
That winter dearth denudes,
Ironstone caves give back the burr
Of lambs in multitudes;

Grass waves again where drought
Bleached every upland kraal;
A peach-tree shoots along the wind
Pink volleys through a broken wall.

And willows growing round the dam
May now be seen
With all their traceries of twigs
Just hesitating to be green,

Soon to be hung with colonies
All swaying with the leaves
Of pendant wicker love-nests
The pretty loxia weaves.

A LEVANTINE

A mouth like old silk soft with use,
The weak chin of a dying race,
Eyes that know all and look at naught—
    Disease, depravity, disgrace
    Are all united in that face.

And yet the triumph of decay
Outbraves the pride of bouncing fools—
As an old craftsman smiles to hear
       His name respected in the schools
       And sees the rust upon his tools;

Through shades of truth and memory
He burrows, secret as a mole,
And smiles with loose and withered lips
       Because the workings of his soul
       Will, when he's low, stay sound and whole.

With Socrates as ancestor,
And rich Byzantium in his veins,
What if this weakling does not work?
       He never takes the slightest pains
       To exercise his drowsy brains,

But drinks his coffee, smokes and yawns
While new-rich empires rise and fall:
His blood is bluer than their heaven,
       Poor, but no poorer than them all,
       He has no principles at all.

THE CALEDONIAN MARKET

A work-basket made of an old armadillo
    Lined with pink satin now rotten with age,
A novel entitled *The Ostracized Vicar*
    (A spider squashed flat on the title-page),
A faded album of nineteen-o-seven
    Snapshots (now like very weak tea)
Showing high-collared knuts and girls expectant
    In big muslin hats at Bexhill-on-Sea,
A gaselier made of hand-beaten copper
    In the once modern style known as *art nouveau*,
An assegai, and a china slipper,
    And *What a Young Scoutmaster Ought to Know*. .

Who stood their umbrellas in elephants' feet?
    Who hung their hats on the horns of a moose?
Who crossed the ocean with amulets made
    To be hung round the neck of an ailing papoose?

Who paid her calls with a sandalwood card-case?
  From whose eighteen-inch waist hung that thin chatelaine?
Who smoked that meerschaum? Who won that medal?
  That extraordinary vase was evolved by what brain?
Who worked in wool the convolvulus bell-pull?
  Who smiled with those false teeth? Who wore that wig?
Who had that hair-tidy hung by her mirror?
  Whose was the scent-bottle shaped like a pig?

Where are the lads in their tight Norfolk jackets
  Who roistered in pubs that stayed open all day?
Where are the girls in their much tighter corsets
  And where are the figures they loved to display?
Where the old maids in their bric-a-brac settings
  With parlourmaids bringing them dinners and teas?
Where are their counterparts, idle old roués,
  Sodden old bachelors living at ease?
Where the big families, big with possessions,
  Their standards of living, their errors of taste?
Here are the soup-tureens—where is the ambience,
  Arrogance, confidence, hope without haste?

Laugh if you like at this monstrous detritus
  Of middle-class life in the liberal past,
The platypus stuffed, and the frightful epergne.
  You, who are now overtaxed and declassed,
Laugh while you can, for the time may come round
  When the rubbish *you* treasure will lie in this place—
Your wireless set (bust), your ridiculous hats,
  And the photographs of your period face.
Your best-selling novels, your 'functional' chairs,
  Your primitive comforts and notions of style
Are just so much fodder for dealers in junk—
  Let us hope that they'll make your grandchildren smile.

THE PRIZE CAT

Pure blood domestic, guaranteed,   E. J.
Soft-mannered, musical in purr,   Pratt
The ribbon had declared the breed,
Gentility was in the fur.

131

Such feline culture in the gads
No anger ever arched her back—
What distance since those velvet pads
Departed from the leopard's track!

And when I mused how Time had thinned
The jungle strains within the cells,
How human hands had disciplined
Those prowling optic parallels;

I saw the generations pass
Along the reflex of a spring,
A bird had rustled in the grass,
The tab had caught it on the wing:

Behind the leap so furtive-wild
Was such ignition in the gleam,
I thought an Abyssinian child
Had cried out in the whitethroat's scream.

JULY

John
Pudney

A secret is the burden of the stream:
A broth of honeysuckle confidence
From lolling hedges whispers to the sense:
And elms conspiratorially dream.
I walk in all my summers, in immense
Noon-halted time. The sun lights overhead
On roofs of vaulted air, and cloud off-shed
And rinsed. Within the singleness of this suspense
The body crowds alone: my thought is fled
Across horizons infinitely wide.
Child's sin and manly innocence collide
Within the summer standstill of my head.
So shall I count beneath my breath who died,
How many in a moment pass me dead?

PIAZZA PIECE

John Crowe
Ransom

—I am a gentleman in a dustcoat trying
To make you hear. Your ears are soft and small
And listen to an old man not at all,
They want the young men's whispering and sighing.

But see the roses on your trellis dying
And hear the spectral singing of the moon;
For I must have my lovely lady soon,
I am a gentleman in a dustcoat trying.

—I am a lady young in beauty waiting
Until my true love comes, and then we kiss.
But what grey man among the vines is this
Whose words are dry and faint as in a dream?
Back from my trellis, Sir, before I scream!
I am a lady young in beauty waiting.

EPITAPH

Yes yes
and ever it will come to this:
Life folds like a fan with a click!
The hand that lately beat the air
with an arch of painted silk
falls listless in the lap.

The air
the agitation and the flush
close and collapse. A rigid frame
restricts the limbs that once ran free
across the hearth across the fields
over the threatening hills.

*Herbert
Read*

LESSONS OF THE WAR
To Alan Michell
*Vixi duellis nuper idoneus
Et militavi non sine gloria*

1. Naming of Parts

Today we have naming of parts. Yesterday,
We had daily cleaning. And tomorrow morning,
We shall have what to do after firing. But today,
Today we have naming of parts. Japonica
Glistens like coral in all of the neighbouring gardens,
    And today we have naming of parts.

*Henry
Reed*

This is the lower sling swivel. And this
Is the upper sling swivel, whose use you will see,
When you are given your slings. And this is the piling swivel,
Which in your case you have not got. The branches
Hold in the gardens their silent, eloquent gestures,
    Which in our case we have not got.

This is the safety-catch, which is always released
With an easy flick of the thumb. And please do not let me
See anyone using his finger. You can do it quite easy
If you have any strength in your thumb. The blossoms
Are fragile and motionless, never letting anyone see
    Any of them using their finger.

And this you can see is the bolt. The purpose of this
Is to open the breech, as you see. We can slide it
Rapidly backwards and forwards: we call this
Easing the spring. And rapidly backwards and forwards
The early bees are assaulting and fumbling the flowers:
    They call it easing the Spring.

They call it easing the Spring: it is perfectly easy
If you have any strength in your thumb: like the bolt,
And the breech, and the cocking-piece, and the point of balance,
Which in our case we have not got; and the almond-blossom
Silent in all of the gardens and the bees going backwards and forwards,
    For today we have naming of parts.

'HAD I PASSION TO MATCH MY SKILL'

James
Reeves

Had I passion to match my skill,
I would not hear the worm complain,
The worm that frets and mumbles still
In the corridors of my brain.

The flames that burn inside my heart,
On what fuel do they feed?
I the secret would impart,
Had I skill to match my need.

Had I passion and skill
To match my daring will,
I would rise and seek
The stony path that scales the virgin peak.

134

Between my hands I hold my brain,
Between my ribs I nurse a fire;
Beyond my utmost step remain
The summits where the goats aspire.

Inside my brain the worm revolves,
The heart consumes inside my breast;
And so I sit, and nothing solves
The puzzles that are not expressed:

While at my feet old Faithful dwells,
Stretched out with one dull eye ajar,
A nose that forages for smells,
A tongue that moves from scar to scar.

LEAVING TOWN

It was impossible to leave the town.
Bumping across a maze of obsolete rails
Three times we reached the gasworks and reversed.
We could not get away from the canal;
Dead cats, dead hopes in those grey deeps immersed
Over our efforts breathed a spectral prayer.
The cattle-market and the gospel-hall
Returned like fictions of our own despair,
And like Hesperides the suburbs seemed,
Shining far off towards the guiltless fields.
We finished in a little *cul-de-sac*
Where on the pavement sat a ragged girl
Mourning beside a jug-and-bottle entrance.
Once more we turned the car and started back.

'THIS IS YOUR ELEGY'

This is your elegy, the grey sea grieving—
This and the gulls' disconsolate reply.
Beyond your hearing is their derelict cry.

Now every wave reminds me of your leaving.
There is no houseless bird more lost than I.
This is your elegy, the grey sea grieving—
This and the gulls' disconsolate reply.

To end your absence and your unbelieving
With yet one more 'I love you', I would try
To call my sea-bird back from the cold sky.
This is your elegy, the grey sea grieving—
This and the gulls' disconsolate reply.
Beyond your hearing is their derelict cry.

THE FLIGHT OF THE GEESE

Charles G. D.
Roberts

I hear the low wind wash the softening snow,
    The low tide loiter down the shore. The night
    Full filled with April forecast, hath no light.
The salt wave on the sedge-flat pulses slow.
Through the hid furrows lisp in murmurous flow
    The thaw's shy ministers; and hark! The height
    Of heaven grows weird and loud with unseen flight
Of strong hosts prophesying as they go!
High through the drenched and hollow night their wings
    Beat northward hard on winter's trail. The sound
Of their confused and solemn voices, borne
Athwart the dark to their long Arctic morn,
    Comes with a sanction and an awe profound,
A boding of unknown, foreshadowed things.

THE HARVEST FIELD

W. R.
Rodgers

There is nothing to note; only the mowers
Moving like doom. Slowly, one by one,
A gloom of bees rises and soon snores
Thunder-headed away into the sun.

Listen! Listen! do you hear the hiss
Of the scythe in the long grasses
That are silently tingling like bells that kiss
And repel as the wind passes.

There in the last care and core of corn
The hare is couched: not till the mowers flash
Their smiling scythes, and all its walls are shorn
Will the wild creature dash
Into the wintry air of hound and horn.

Listen! Listen! do you hear the hiss
Of the scythe in the long grasses of your laughter?
More is mowed than you know, for this
Is Time's swathe, and you are the one that he's after.

THE JOURNEY OF THE MAGI

Behold there came wise men from the east,
saying, Where is he, for we have seen his star?

It was a dark January night, cold and snowing
When the Three Kings started out
On their annual journey: and what on earth
They were doing—and such a time to be going!
And, honestly, what it was all about
Not one of them knew. But they wanted a birth,
A new life, as we all do. Was the journey wise?—
Yes, or No? Well, that was anybody's guess
As it still is: a risk. A different address
May only land you in a different kind of a mess.
Put it no higher than that. But still, there was the Star
Throbbing in front like a bell, bobbing them on from afar,
Regardless of hail, rain, or snow, or glitter or glare.
The Three Kings marched away into the west,
To one dark enterprise they were addressed.
There was nowhere they would not go, feast or fast,
Slum or salon, bethel or brothel, if only at last
And at ease they could come to the truth and be blessed.
Perhaps in some far corner of the world
An answer lay, a sleeping past was curled.
February now, the driving swathes of rain
Swaddle the hills that edge the Atlantic main,
And wave on wave like superimposing hands
Slip and withdraw on Europe's farthest strands.
Through the wet night the Three Kings rode away,
It mattered not who called on them to stay;
It matters not who dances or who sings
They must away to find the King of Kings.
To welcome gravity, and to forego fun
Is still their fate who seek the heavenly One
And choose the Star.

And now the month is March,
Bloodbursty buds are pink upon the larch.
One thing about journeys which is rather good
—Things never happen how and where they should.
God, for example, as the Three Kings found,
Is seldom above-board, but underground;
And on the other hand, the Devil
Is to be met on almost every level,
High place and holy day. The guide-book's Star
Has small relation to things as they are.
Still, one lives and learns that saints, if fat,
Are none the earthier or the worse for that;
God can be sought for in a golden rain
Of levity and fireworks; piety's not pain.
The guns go off, the rockets fly
Over the Kings now riding by.
In passing, one may duly note
That reverence need not choke the throat
Or dull the cheek.
It's only those
Who hug the sober truth, the gloomy ones,
Who always fear to let off their guns.
Truth's never sober, but, like a wayward gipsy
She wears the loudest colours, shouts, and goes half-tipsy.
Now up, now down, now gay, now melancholy,
Now drawn to hope and now pursued by folly,
The Three Kings marched zigzag, a star their brolly.
Caspar got blind one night, Melchior met a lady,
Balthazar was involved in something shady;
Strange that, in lands, and countries quite unknown,
We find, not others' strangeness, but our own;
That is one use of journeys; if one delves,
Differently, one's sure to find one's selves.
O in what wildernesses of one another
We wander looking for ourselves! What bother
We go through, what cold, what heat
To find the answer up our own back street.
Meanwhile this gipsy life the Three Kings led, as unconfined

As the May bloom that blithely takes the wind.
A man comes to the Three Kings and cries
'I'm an insurance agent; I advise—
In case you're tempted, sirs, to trust your eyes—
Take out a policy, against surprise.
Seeing's believing; journeys are dangerous things;

Belief can lay its icy hand on Kings.
For a small premium we will give relief
In case of sickness, second sight, belief;
But if at sixty-five you're still quite blind,
You'll get a bonus; our company's that kind.
Just answer these few questions:—Have you had
Father or Mother who was ill or mad
Or bad enough to see things as they are?
Did any of your family see a star?
Barring that—' With that they pushed the man away;
Live dangerously, see all, and come what may,
Was their belief.
The Three Kings hitched their wagon to the Star
And gave the Star its head. Now near, now far,
Now in, now out, now to and fro it led;
Never straight. Journeys are always curly,
Like comets or like hairpins they are meant
To crown or to lead up to some event.
Herod did all he could do to prevent
Their coming. This journey had its hazards.
He broke the poles, and he cut the wires,
He stole their pump and deflated their tyres,
And he turned their messengers into liars;
But in vain.
He muffled the knocker, disconnected the bell,
Turned up his radio till it howled like hell,
Changed his name and address as well;
But in vain.

After October with its fiery leaf
Came grey November, frozen, as in grief;
Dumpy with impotence King Herod sat,
Not even bothering to take off his hat,
When in came the Three Kings, as if by chance,
And Herod rose and made great song and dance
About them. Black Caspar said to Balthazar
'He's a good sort, Herod; there's no colour-bar
With him.' 'May be,' said Melchior, 'but why
Does he keep staring up into the sky?
And why's he quizzing us about the Star?'
'O just some complex,' Caspar said, 'to do with power:
Rank has its obligations, and in fact
The first is to preserve itself intact.'
—So they argued on, intent;

Till suddenly, above the Palace towers
They saw their guiding star turn red, like Mars,
And knew that it was angry. Bloody wars
It threatened. And at once they went
Without good-byes.

December now; the Three Kings stood
Benighted in the deepest wood,
The wits-end of their hardihood.
No longer kings, but helpless now
They threw away their golden bough;
They stamped upon their golden crowns
And damned the country, damned the towns.
They'd lost the Star, their only link
And anchor-light. O not a blink
No hope, no help in earth or sky!
—They gave a last despairing cry.
Then suddenly all raised a shout
For overhead the Star flared out
Just like a fan: and there they saw
In the last ditch, on the last straw,
In front of them a heavenly child.
See! it looked up at them and smiled.
It was the child within themselves
For which they'd sought, for which Age delves
—Now Age and Innocence can meet,
Now, now the circle is complete,
The journey's done. Lord, Lord, how sweet!

NIGHT PATROL

*Alan
Ross*

We sail at dusk. The red moon,
Rising in a paper lantern, sets fire
To the water, the black headland disappears,
Sullen in shadow, clenched like a paw.

The docks grow flat, rubbered with mist.
Cranes, like tall drunks, hang
Over the railway. The unloading of coal
Continues under blue arc-lights.

Turning south, the moon like a rouged face
Between masts, the knotted aerials swing
Taut against the horizon, the bag
Of sea crumpled in the spray-flecked blackness.

Towards midnight the cold stars, high
Over Europe, freeze on the sky,
Stigmata above the flickering lights
Of Holland. Flashes of gunfire

Lick out over meditative coastlines, betraying
The stillness. Taking up position, night falls
Exhausted about us. The wakes
Of gunboats sew the green dark with speed.

From Dunkirk red flames open fanwise
In spokes of light; like the rising moon
Setting fire to the sky, the remote
Image of death burns on the water.

The slow muffle of hours. Clouds grow visible.
Altering course the moon congeals on a new
Bearing. Northwards again, and Europe recedes
With the first sharp splinters of dawn.

The orange sky lies over the harbour,
Derricks and pylons like scarecrows
Black in the early light. And minesweepers
Pass us, moving out slowly to the North Sea.

SURVIVORS

With the ship burning in their eyes
The white faces float like refuse
In the darkness—the water screwing
Oily circles where the hot steel lies.

They clutch with fingers frozen into claws
The lifebelts thrown from a destroyer,
And see, between the future's doors,
The gasping entrance of the sea.

Taken on board as many as lived, who
Had a mind left for living and the ocean,
They open eyes running with surf,
Heavy with the grey ghosts of explosion.

The meaning is not yet clear,
Where daybreak died in the smile—
And the mouth remained stiff
And grinning, stupid for a little while.

But soon they joke, easy and warm
As men will who have died once
Yet somehow were able to find their way—
Muttering this was not included in their pay.

Later, sleepless at night, the brain spinning
With cracked images, they won't forget
The confusion and the oily dead,
Nor yet the casual knack of living.

AUTUMN IN HYDE PARK

The beeches' copper islands float
Suspended in the mellow woods,
Where autumn substitutes for words
A private dictionary of moods.

The red and russet-throated birds
Describe in avenues of love
Circles of a yellow grief
Narrowed in the plane tree's leaf.

The rowan's scarlet statement burns
A sudden presage of the doom
That strips the naked falling bark
White in the amber gloom.

The lake conveys the quiet pause
Between the sable splash of oars,
As underfoot the horses' hooves
Trample the images of larks.

The evening's traffic soon dilates
Smoky spirals in its lights,
And twists the plaster-coloured
Mist into honeyed fumes of night.

Then ruins echo unheard noise
As darkness drifts like tepid breath,
Printing on the season's hearse
The black letters of its death.

ZOO

The smell assaults you first, from places
Where nightly the padded steps rehearse
Africa's movements in its restless sleep.
Here all our captive faults are nursed
Brooding in their sultry paces.

Like phrases they turn and reiterate
Lost meanings in their striped and alien cages,
Pausing to blink a heavy eye at sun
That curls up the pallid ends of pages
In their history blanked-out and done.

Now nothing remains in this sullen world
Where always on a straw-laid floor
They meditate, like prisoners in a war
Fought for lost causes, whose mere act
Of living forced them to participate.

Ignorant of ends and means, knowing
Only the blank reality of exile, they seek
The one vivid proof of life, their shadow
That alone answers when they speak—
A familiar guardian whom, a little way behind, they tow.

Watching, we turn our backs and move away,
Suddenly ashamed and moved by some glint
Of pity in their shooting eyes, as if today
They showed some symptom or some hint
Of our predicament tomorrow, or the next day.

BASRA: EXPERIMENT WITH OIL

Oilwells and palms; the silver tassels of pylons; dhows
Adrift on olive and gilded water, like carcasses of birds
Whose wings are blown into sails; banks of buffalo
Testing the sluggish current; boats embedded in reeds,

With patches of startling green round the trunks
Of the date-trees—round all these the afternoon sinks
And curdles, a fringed ochre-stained landscape of junk.

Villages of mud, like plasticine models are clamped
Over leaking shores, where, for miles, only flatness exudes
Sumptuous avenues of dirt, and the skyline is stamped
With the frescoing smoke of the docks. Heavily, broods
Of pelican and crane take off from the marshes;
Beyond them, aeroplanes come in over wheatfields in flood.
Now they've found oil, cracked smiles in the desert break
Through the gravel; steel-drills, like flowers, grow
Adjacent to mud; and only unworldly griefs are at stake.

SPRING IN GROVE ALLEY

A. L.
Rowse

Spring comes: the sudden ashamed sun bursts out
Over the roofs, and Grove Alley is dramatized
With ribbed shadows and lights at tangent.
The old lady with the worm-eaten fur
And tame cat obsequious, bitten of the mange,
Is at her area-gate, sniffing the morning air.
The milk-cans at the door are squalid, platitudinous.
A thrush to the imprisoning walls is eloquent.
At the bend of the road the street-lamp leans
With the times, out of joint.
The railings are there as before:
So is the old lady of the fur,
And the mangy cat,
So is the sudden sun,
So is the Spring.

From *The Land*

Victoria
Sackville-West

The country habit has me by the heart,
For he's bewitched forever who has seen,
Not with his eyes but with his vision, Spring
Flow down the woods and stipple leaves with sun,
As each man knows the life that fits him best,
The shape it makes in his soul, the tune, the tone,

And after ranging on a tentative flight
Stoops like the merlin to the constant lure.
The country habit has me by the heart.
I never hear the sheep-bells in the fold,
Nor see the ungainly heron rise and flap
Over the marsh, nor hear the asprous corn
Clash, as the reapers set the sheaves in shocks
(That like a tented army dream away
The night beneath the moon in silvered fields),
Nor watch the stubborn team of horse and man
Graven upon the skyline, nor regain
The sign-posts on the roads towards my home
Bearing familiar names—without a strong
Leaping of recognition; only here
Lies peace beyond uneasy truancy;
Here meet and marry many harmonies,
—All harmonies being ultimately one,—
Small mirroring majestic; for as earth
Rolls on her journey, so her little fields
Ripen or sleep, and the necessities
Of seasons match the planetary law.
So truly stride between the earth and heaven
Sowers of grain; so truly in the spring
Earth's orbit swings both blood and sap to rhythm,
And infinite and humble are at one;
So the brown hedger, through the evening lanes
Homeward returning, sees above the ricks,
Sickle in hand, the sickle in the sky.

The Land—lines from 'WINTER'

Hear next of winter, when the florid summer,
The bright barbarian scarfed in a swathe of flowers,
The corn a golden ear-ring on her cheek,
Has left our north to winter's finer etching,
To raw-boned winter, when the sun
Slinks in a narrow and furtive arc,
Red as the harvest moon, from east to west,
And the swans go home at dusk to the leaden lake
Dark in the plains of snow.

Water alone remains untouched by snow.

Victoria
Sackville-West

Here is no colour, here but form and structure,
The bones of trees, the magpie bark of birches,
A pse of trees and tracery of network,
Fields of snow and tranquil trees in snow
Through veils of twilight, northern, still, and sad,
Waiting for night, and for the moon
Riding the sky and turning snow to beauty,
Pale in herself as winter's very genius,
Casting the shadows delicate of trees,
Moon-shadows on the moon-lit snow, the ghost
Of shadows, veering with the moving moon,
Faint as the markings on the silver coin
Risen in heaven,—shades of barren ranges,
Craters, and lunar Apennines, and plains
Old as the earth, and cold as space, and empty,
Whence Earth appears a planet far surpassing
Our ken of any star for neighbouring splendour,
Her continents, her seas, her mountain ranges
Splendid and visible, majestic planet
Sweeping through space, and bearing in her train
Her silver satellite that sees no strife,
No warring of her men, no grief, no anger,
No blood spilt red to stain the golden planet,
But sees her architecture royally:
Dark Asia; islands; spread of the Pacific,
The silver satellite that casts the ghost
Of ghostly trees across the fields of snow.

Now in the radiant night no men are stirring:
The little houses sleep with shuttered panes;
Only the hares are wakeful, loosely loping
Along the hedges with their easy gait,
And big loose ears, and pad-prints crossing snow;
The ricks and trees stand silent in the moon,
Loaded with snow, and tiny drifts from branches
Slip to the ground in woods with sliding sigh.
Private the woods, enjoying a secret beauty.

The Land—lines from 'SPRING'

That was a spring of storms. They prowled the night;
Low level lightning flickered in the east
Continuous. The white pear-blossom gleamed
Motionless in the flashes; birds were still;

Darkness and silence knotted to suspense,
Riven by the premonitory glint
Of skulking storm, a giant that whirled a sword
Over the low horizon, and with tread
Earth-shaking ever threatened his approach,
But to delay his terror kept afar,
And held earth stayed in waiting like a beast
Bowed to receive a blow. But when he strode
Down from his throne of hills upon the plain,
And broke his anger to a thousand shards
Over the prostrate fields, then leapt the earth
Proud to accept his challenge; drank his rain;
Under his sudden wind tossed wild her trees;
Opened her secret bosom to his shafts;
The great drops spattered; then above the house
Crashed thunder, and the little wainscot shook
And the green garden in the lightning lay.

The Garden—lines from 'WINTER'

Beauty's not always in a scarlet robe.
She wears an old black shawl;
She flouts the flesh and shows the bone
When winter trees are tall.
More beautiful than fact may be
The shadow on the wall.

Beauty's not always prinked in all her vaunt;
It pleases her to speak
In basic whisper to an ear
That will not find her bleak;
The hearing ear, the seeing eye
Who catch her signs oblique.

Oh, fairer than young harlot Summer proud
This subtle, crooked, wise
Old Winter creaks a different truth
Scorning the sensuous lies;
Etches the finer skeleton
For more perceptive eyes.

147

The Garden—lines from 'SUMMER'

There's not a rhyme to *wasp* in English tongue.
Poor wasp, unloved unsung!
Only the homely proverb celebrates
These little dragons of the summer day
That each man hates.
'Wasps haunt the honey-pot,' they say,
Or 'Put your hand into a wasps' nest,' thus
Neatly condensing all report for us
By sharp experience into wisdom stung,
As in the proverb's way.

> *Of many a man it might be said*
> *No one loved him till he was dead,*
> *But of a wasp not even then*
> *As it is said of many men.*

Dug by nocturnal badger from his nest;
Branded, as though by his own stripes, a pest;
Every man's hand against him, every dog
Snapping mid-air with fine heraldic leap
Between a summer sleep and summer sleep
On drowsy, drenched, and lotus afternoon
When peaches ripen and the ring-doves croon.

So let me write the wasp his apologue
In blend of hatred, wonder, and of jest;
That moral fable never told
Of little Satan in his black and gold,
His coat of tigerskin;
Fastened, a close, a dreamy glutton lover
Drinking late fig and later nectarine.
Let me discover
Some evil beauty in his striped array,
Bad angel of the winged air-borne tribe,
And have the honour of his earliest scribe.

Evil he is; to him was evil given
If evil be within our judgement, when
We seek to sift the purposes of heaven.
Exquisite wasp! that our fine fruit devours,
His taste at least as elegant as ours.
And if he should not strike at meddling men
Why did his Maker arm him with a sting?

He's small, he's vicious, he's an easy prey;
With greater skill our ingenuity
Kills with one crack so intricate a thing;
So difficult to make, beyond our powers.
Man can make man, but there his cunning ends.
That necessary act he can dispatch
As Nature urges, launching out a batch
Of new descendants, rivals, precious friends,
But not an insect subtle on the wing.

PREHISTORIC BURIALS

These barrows of the century-darkened dead,—   *Siegfried*
Memorials of oblivion, these turfed tombs   *Sassoon*
Of muttering ancestries whose fires, once red,
Now burn for me beyond mysterious glooms;
I pass them day by day while daylight fills
My sense of sight on these time-haunted hills.

Could I but watch those burials that began
Whole history—flint and bronze and iron beginnings,
When under this wide Wiltshire sky crude man
Warred with his world and augured our world-winnings!
Could I but enter that unholpen brain,
Cabined and comfortless and insecure,
That ruled some settlement on Salisbury Plain
And offered blood to blind primeval powers,—
Dim Caliban whose doom was to endure
Earth's ignorant nullity made strange with flowers.

ANTIQUITIES

Enormous aqueducts have had their day,
And moles make mounds where marshals camped and clashed.
On stones where awe-struck emperors knelt to pray
The tourist gapes with guide-book, unabashed.
Historian Time, who in his 'Life of Man'
Records the whole, himself is much unread:
The breath must go from beauty, and the span
Of Lethe bleaken over all the dead.

Only the shattered arch remains to tell
Humanity its transience and to be
Life-work for archaeologists who spell
The carven hieroglyphics of Chaldee.
And where the toiling town once seethed in smoke
There'll drop, through quiet, one acorn from an oak.

GLORIA MUNDI

Who needs words in autumn woods
When colour concludes decay?
There old stories are told in glories
For winds to scatter away.

Wisdom narrows where downland barrows
Image the world's endeavour.
There time's tales are as light that fails
On faces fading forever.

EARLY CHRONOLOGY

Slowly the daylight left our listening faces.

Professor Brown with level baritone
Discoursed into the dusk.
                              Five thousand years
He guided us through scientific spaces
Of excavated History; till his lone
Roads of research grew blurred; and in our ears
Time was the rumoured tongues of vanished races,
And Thought a chartless Age of Ice and Stone.

The story ended: and the darkened air
Flowered while he lit his pipe; an aureole glowed
Enwreathed with smoke: the moment's match-light showed
His rosy face, broad brow, and smooth grey hair,
Backed by the crowded book-shelves.
                              In his wake
An archaeologist began to make
Assumptions about aqueducts (he quoted
Professor Sandstorm's book); and soon they floated
Through desiccated forests; mangled myths;
And argued easily round megaliths.

Beyond the college garden something glinted;
A copper moon climbed clear above black trees.
Some Lydian coin? . . . Professor Brown agrees
That copper coins *were* in that Culture minted.
But, as her whitening way aloft she took,
I thought she had a pre-dynastic look.

SONNET

Vernon
Scannell

So you have come to scorn the works of God
When shaping images for future eyes;
Now you have left the ancient paths they trod,
They whose great songs amazed impartial skies.
Yet still you cry beneath the same fierce whips
Of hatred, envy, love; yet still you pray
To similar Gods as they; but your pale lips
Are sealed, your hands mould perishable clay.
You see eternity reflected here,
In this proud monster built of shining steel:
It is as transient as a single tear
Or dying echo of a church-bell's peal.
Look now, for still about Ophelia's grave
The opalescent flowers hold sad conclave.

SCHOOLROOM ON A WET AFTERNOON

The unrelated paragraphs of morning
Are forgotten now: the severed heads of kings
Rot by the misty Thames: the rose of York
And Lancaster are pressed between the leaves
Of history; negroes sleep in Africa.
The complexities of simple interest lurk
In inkwells and the brittle sticks of chalk:
Afternoon is come and English Grammar.

Rain falls as though the sky has been bereaved,
Stutters its inarticulate grief on glass
Of every lachrymose pane. The children read
Their books or make pretence of concentration,
Each bowed head seems bent in supplication
Or resignation to the fate that waits
In the unmapped forests of the future.
Is it their doomed innocence noon weeps for?

In each diminutive breast a human heart
Pumps out the necessary blood: desires,
Pains and ecstasies surfride each singing wave
Which breaks in darkness on the mental shores.
Each child is disciplined; absorbed and still
At his small desk. Yet lift the lid and see,
Amidst frayed books and pencils, other shapes:
Vicious rope, glaring blade, the gun cocked to kill.

CANTERBURY IN WINTER

Francis
Scarfe

Winter wind through city trees and towers
is song in motion, mass invisible
ruffling the pattern of the kneeling streets,
bearing the old bell-voices, English voices
of craftsmen, peasants, echoing their beliefs
with overtones of kings and choirs and priests

No pilgrim now stands humble in the dark
nor sleeps familiar by a martyr's grave,
nor longs towards the spires and gargoyles set
upon a nation's monument, nor prays
to live and die here: that innocence is gone
when travellers knelt to kiss the Kentish stone

But still through burning glass the sun and moon
interpret what is spoken by the bells;
and still the simple story stains the floor
with images of martyred lives, where one
dropped blood and cried, and still his wounded ghost
rebukes the saved, the indifferent, and the lost.

THE INARTICULATE

Howard
Sergeant

His name was never mentioned in despatches,
nor was he hero of the desperate stand.
His death obscured no headlines, roused no snatches
of sympathy or personal sense of loss
even in comrade hearts. Under strict command
of parent, schoolmaster, and caustic boss,
his mind and limbs were harnessed to the clock;
and all his hours were blossoms for others to tread.
He gathered experience from the books he read,
and clambered mountains with a dreamer's alpenstock.

From attic windows he watched the white rains falling
but lacked the sounding-thought to fathom flood.
His was the voice of the lonely seagull calling
over the roof-tops to winds and an empty sky.
He sought no revelation in unfolding bud;
nor claimed a nobler cause for which to die
than the accidental bursting of a gun:
so little song or colour to warrant his remaining—
yet one there was for whom his life held meaning,
and with his passing, grief walled up the sun.

INTERVENTION

Outside, Orion strides indifferent and cool.
   Impulsive winds disturb the scents
Of feeding animals, and stir the drinking-pool
   To silent laughter. Farm implements
And gear, loosely scattered around the farmyard wall,
   Assume a beauty not their own
Beneath sly wizardry of moon, whose random call
   Can make a star of moistened stone,
A spiral incantation from a coil of wire,
   And armoured knights of three milk-churns.

Here in the cosy farmhouse, by a cheerful fire,
   We gossip; conversation turns
To the capricious ways of Nature, and vast wealth
   Of country lore shyly concealed
From all but faithful lovers of the land; the health
   Of new-born calves; birds of the field;
And the value of heifers. I feel at peace, sincere
   In sharing the intimate views
Of these countryfolk—what seems unnatural is to hear,
   At nine o'clock, the radio news.

NOT WAVING BUT DROWNING

Nobody heard him, the dead man,   *Stevie*
But still he lay moaning: *Smith*
I was much further out than you thought
And not waving but drowning.

Poor chap, he always loved larking
And now he's dead
It must have been too cold for him his heart gave way,
They said.

Oh, no no no, it was too cold always
(Still the dead one lay moaning)
I was much too far out all my life
And not waving but drowning.

PYLONS

*Stanley
Snaith*

Over the tree'd upland evenly striding,
One after one they lift their serious shapes
That ring with light. The statement of their steel
Contradicts nature's softer architecture.
Earth will not accept them as it accepts
A wall, a plough, a church so coloured of earth
It might be some experiment of the soils.
Yet are they outposts of the trekking future.
Into the thatch-hung consciousness of hamlets
They blaze new thoughts, new habits.
                                    Traditions
Are being trod down like flowers dropped by children.
Already that farm boy striding and throwing seed
In the shoulder-hinged half-circle Millet knew,
Looks grey with antiquity as his dead forebears,
A half familiar figure out of the Georgics,
Unheeded by these new-world, rational towers.

TO SOME BUILDERS OF CITIES

You have thrust Nature out, to make
A wilderness where nothing grows
But forest of unbudding stone
(The sparrow's lonely for his boughs);
You fling up citadels to stay
The soft invasion of the rose.

But though you put the earth in thrall
And ransack all her fragrant dowers,
Her old accomplice, Heaven, will plot
To take with stars your roofs and towers;
And neither stone nor steel can foil
That ambuscade of midnight flowers.

BASE TOWN

Winter's white guard continual on the hills;   *Bernard*
The wind savaging from the stony valleys   *Spencer*
And the unseen front. And always the soldiers going,
Soldiers and lorries beating the streets of cobble,
Like blood to where a wound is flowing.

War took friends, lights and names away. Clapped down
Shutters on windows' welcome. Brought those letters
Which wished to say so much they dared not say.
The proud and feminine ships in the harbour roads
Turned to a North-East grey.

Curious the intimacy we felt with Them;
We moved our meals to fit Their raids; we read
Their very hand across each bomb-slashed wall.
Their charred plane fallen in the cratered square
Held twisted in it all

Their work, Their hate, Their failure. Prisoners
Bearded and filthy, had bones, eyes and hair
Like other men in need. But dead like snow,
Cold like those racing winds or sirens' grief,
Was the hate which struck no blow:

The fear of speaking was a kind of tic
Pulling at the eyes. If stranger drank with stranger
It seemed thief drank with thief. Was it only every
Night, the fall of the early and lampless dark?
I remember it so often. And the lie,
The twist of reason,
The clever rumour planted in the nerves,
The dossier infecting like a coccus;
All these became for us the town, the season.

These, and the knowledge that to die,
Some stony miles north of our wintering
Was a more ordinary thing.

OLIVE TREES

The dour thing in olive trees
is that their trunks are stooped like never dying crones,
and they camp where roads climb, and drink with dust and stones.

The pleasant thing is how in the heat
their plumage brushes the sight with a bird's wing feeling:
and perhaps the gold of their oil is mild with dreams of healing.

The cold thing is how they were
there at the start of us; and one grey look surveyed
the builder imagining the city, the historian with his spade.

The warm thing is that they are
first promise of the South to waking travellers:
of the peacock sea, and the islands and their boulder-lumbered spurs.

AN ELEMENTARY SCHOOL CLASS ROOM IN A SLUM

Stephen
Spender

Far far from gusty waves these children's faces.
Like rootless weeds, the hair torn round their pallor.
The tall girl with her weighed-down head. The paper-
seeming boy, with rat's eyes. The stunted, unlucky heir
Of twisted bones, reciting a father's gnarled disease,
His lesson from his desk. At back of the dim class
One unnoted, sweet and young. His eyes live in a dream
Of squirrel's game, in tree room, other than this.

On sour cream walls, donations. Shakespeare's head,
Cloudless at dawn, civilized dome riding all cities.
Belled, flowery, Tyrolese valley. Open-handed map
Awarding the world its world. And yet, for these
Children, these windows, not this world, are world,
Where all their future's painted with a fog,
A narrow street sealed in with a lead sky,
Far far from rivers, capes, and stars of words.

Surely, Shakespeare is wicked, the map a bad example
With ships and sun and love tempting them to steal—
For lives that slyly turn in their cramped holes
From fog to endless night? On their slag heap, these children
Wear skins peeped through by bones and spectacles of steel
With mended glass, like bottle bits on stones.
All of their time and space are foggy slum.
So blot their maps with slums as big as doom.

Unless, governor, teacher, inspector, visitor,
This map becomes their window and these windows
That shut upon their lives like catacombs,
Break O break open till they break the town
And show the children to green fields, and all their world
Run azure on gold sands, to let their tongues
Run naked into books, the white and green leaves open
History theirs whose language is the sun.

THE PYLONS

The secret of these hills was stone, and cottages
Of that stone made,
And crumbling roads
That turned on sudden hidden villages.

Now over these small hills, they have built the concrete
That trails black wire;
Pylons, those pillars
Bare like nude giant girls that have no secret.

The valley with its gilt and evening look
And the green chestnut
Of customary root,
Are mocked dry like the parched bed of a brook.

But far above and far as sight endures
Like whips of anger
With lightning's danger
There runs the quick perspective of the future.

This dwarfs our emerald country by its trek
So tall with prophecy:
Dreaming of cities
Where often clouds shall lean their swan-white neck.

I HEAR THE CRIES OF EVENING'

I hear the cries of evening, while the paw
Of dark, creeps up the turf:
Sheep bleating, swaying gull's cry, the rook's 'Caw',
The hammering surf.

I am inconstant, yet this constancy
Of natural rest, pulls at my heart;
Town-bred, I feel the roots of each earth-cry
Tear me apart.

These are the creakings of the dusty day
When the dog Night bites sharp,
These fingers grip my soul and tear away
And pluck me like a harp.

I feel the huge sphere turn, the great wheel sing
While beasts move to their ease:
Sheep's love, gulls' peace—I feel my chattering
Uncared by these.

THE BARN

Half hidden by trees, the sheer roof of the barn
Is a river of tiles, warped
By winding currents of weather
Suns and storms ago.

Through beech leaves, its vermilion seems
A Red Admiral's wing, with veins
Of lichen and rust, and underwing
Of winter-left leaves.

Now, in the Spring, a sapling's jet
Of new, pure flame, cuts across
The low long gutter. One leaf holds up
Red tiles reflected in its cup.

At the side of the road where cars crash past,
The barn lies under the sky like a throat
Full of dark gurgitation:

A ghost of a noise—a hint of a gust
Caught in the rafters centuries ago:
The creak of winch, the wood turn of a wheel.

Entangled in murmurs, as in a girl's hair,
Is the enthusiastic scent
Of coarse, yellow straw—lit by that sunbeam,
Which, laden with motes, strikes across the floor.

THE SUBMERGED CATHEDRAL, SELSEY

This is the lane, they say. Deserted, lonely,   *Margaret*
Grasses whisper in the wind, dipping their fringes,   *Stanley-Wrench*
The knopped clappers of the knapweed beat
Each on each like drumsticks. Clashing branches
Part to show the blue silk of the sea
Ravelled with white; sometimes its waves invade
The lane, and trample up it like herds of horses,
Leaving a stain of brown, hoof-prints of weed.

Yet once, the peak and summit, crown of the avenue,
Crouched the cathedral, lifting a little spire
Like a shell, and roofed with shingle, set with stones
As if washed up by the tide. Nothing remains,
Not even the faint, dredged echo of the bells,
Or, harsh as tree trunks, broad as boles, the bulk
Of buttresses and pillars thick as thighs
In the aqueous twilight, the trembling innocence

Of the wave, and the moon-green silences of the sea.
The tides have rubbed it, cancelled it out, and sucked it
Into the anonymity of water,
Ground it down, fretted it to sand,
Like a dream crumbling away at the touch of daylight.
Nothing is left: the cold touch of the tides
Hides stones once warm with sunlight, worn by human
Hands, and the fret and print of humble feet.

Driven back by the sea, did they abandon it
To the imperious congregation of water?
Did the waves come shyly, hesitating
Like children daring each other to go inside,
Then white and fresh as a bride, sweep up the aisle
Touching the pews with white, flecked froth of foam,
Flooding into the transepts like a glut of tourists?
And a chancel full of waters, a choir vibrating

With the full swell of the sea praised the Lord
Who made the oceans and all that moved therein.
And swinging in the tower, dragged by their ropes of weed,
The great bells of waves roared through the rafters.
Then, like the sprawling carcase of a whale
Bone-white and dry it lay; around the eaves
Silver fish in shoals moved thick as swallows
Who brush with their dark blue wings our own warm roofs.

Through the arched sockets of the shattered windows
Darted the mackerel, dappled, tabby as taffeta;
A confetti of sprats, a quicksilver smelting of herring
Flashed up the darkened nave, dipped past the altar
In living praise, their grace, their beauty worship,
And through the cloisters, with the quilted pace
Of old, old men, move sole, grey as the stone,
And the leopard plaice, flecked with bright marigold,

Meditating with the lidless stare
Of gargoyle and saint eroded by the sea.
Gone, it is gone. Not even the fisherman's ear
Hears the tidal swing of sunken bells.
Yet in men's minds like the memory of a dream
Haunting the day, the lost cathedral lies,
And they look up, their glance of love a prayer,
Seeing the shadow of that vanished spire.

FERN HILL

Dylan
Thomas

Now as I was young and easy under the apple boughs
About the lilting house and happy as the grass was green,
    The night above the dingle starry,
      Time let me hail and climb
    Golden in the heydays of his eyes,
And honoured among wagons I was prince of the apple towns
And once below a time I lordly had the trees and leaves
      Trail with daisies and barley
    Down the rivers of the windfall light.

And as I was green and carefree, famous among the barns
About the happy yard and singing as the farm was home,
    In the sun that is young once only,
      Time let me play and be
    Golden in the mercy of his means,

And green and golden I was huntsman and herdsman, the calves
Sang to my horn, the foxes on the hills barked clear and cold,
    And the sabbath rang slowly
      In the pebbles of the holy streams.

All the sun long it was running, it was lovely, the hay
Fields high as the house, the tunes from the chimneys, it was air
    And playing, lovely and watery
      And fire green as grass.
    And nightly under the simple stars
As I rode to sleep the owls were bearing the farm away,
All the moon long I heard, blessed among stables, the nightjars
    Flying with the ricks, and the horses
      Flashing into the dark.

And then to awake, and the farm, like a wanderer white
With the dew, come back, the cock on his shoulder: it was all
    Shining, it was Adam and maiden,
      The sky gathered again
    And the sun grew round that very day.
So it must have been after the birth of the simple light
In the first, spinning place, the spellbound horses walking warm
    Out of the whinnying green stable
      On to the fields of praise.

And honoured among foxes and pheasants by the gay house
Under the new made clouds and happy as the heart was long,
    In the sun born over and over,
      I ran my heedless ways,
    My wishes raced through the house high hay
And nothing I cared, at my sky blue trades, that time allows
In all his tuneful turning so few and such morning songs
    Before the children green and golden
      Follow him out of grace,

Nothing I cared, in the lamb white days, that time would take me
Up to the swallow thronged loft by the shadow of my hand,
    In the moon that is always rising,
      Nor that riding to sleep
    I should hear him fly with the high fields
And wake to the farm forever fled from the childless land.
Oh as I was young and easy in the mercy of his means,
    Time held me green and dying
      Though I sang in my chains like the sea.

Dylan
Thomas

Especially when the October wind
With frosty fingers punishes my hair,
Caught by the crabbing sun I walk on fire
And cast a shadow crab upon the land,
By the sea's side, hearing the noise of birds,
Hearing the raven cough in winter sticks,
My busy heart who shudders as she talks
Sheds the syllabic blood and drains her words.

Shut, too, in a tower of words, I mark
On the horizon walking like the trees
The wordy shapes of women, and the rows
Of the star-gestured children in the park,
Some let me make you of the vowelled beeches,
Some of the oaken voices, from the roots
Of many a thorny shire tell you notes,
Some let me make you of the water's speeches.

Behind a pot of ferns the wagging clock
Tells me the hour's word, the neural meaning
Flies on the shafted disk, declaims the morning
And tells the windy weather in the cock.
Some let me make you of the meadow's signs;
The signal grass that tells me all I know
Breaks with the wormy winter through the eye.
Some let me tell you of the raven's sins.

Especially when the October wind
(Some let me make you of autumnal spells,
The spider-tongued, and the loud hill of Wales)
With fists of turnips punishes the land,
Some let me make you of the heartless words.
The heart is drained that, spelling in the scurry
Of chemic blood, warned of the coming fury.
By the sea's side hear the dark-vowelled birds.

DO NOT GO GENTLE INTO THAT
GOOD NIGHT

Do not go gentle into that good night,
Old age should burn and rave at close of day;
Rage, rage against the dying of the light.

Though wise men at their end know dark is right,
Because their words have forked no lightning they
Do not go gentle into that good night.

Good men, the last wave by, crying how bright
Their frail deeds might have danced in a green bay,
Rage, rage against the dying of the light.

Wild men who caught and sang the sun in flight,
And learn, too late, they grieved it on its way,
Do not go gentle into that good night.

Grave men, near death, who see with blinding sight
Blind eyes could blaze like meteors and be gay,
Rage, rage against the dying of the light.

And you, my father, there on the sad height,
Curse, bless, me now with your fierce tears, I pray.
Do not go gentle into that good night.
Rage, rage against the dying of the light.

AND DEATH SHALL HAVE NO DOMINION

And death shall have no dominion.
Dead men naked they shall be one
With the man in the wind and the west moon;
When their bones are picked clean and the clean bones gone,
They shall have stars at elbow and foot;
Though they go mad they shall be sane,
Though they sink through the sea they shall rise again;
Though lovers be lost love shall not;
And death shall have no dominion.

And death shall have no dominion.
Under the windings of the sea
They lying long shall not die windily;
Twisting on racks when sinews give way,
Strapped to a wheel, yet they shall not break;
Faith in their hands shall snap in two,
And the unicorn evils run them through;
Split all ends up they shan't crack;
And death shall have no dominion.

And death shall have no dominion.
No more may gulls cry at their ears
Or waves break loud on the seashores;
Where blew a flower may a flower no more
Lift its head to the blows of the rain;
Though they be mad and dead as nails,
Heads of the characters hammer through daisies;
Break in the sun till the sun breaks down,
And death shall have no dominion.

HOMO SAPIENS 1941

R. S.
Thomas

Murmuration of engines in the cold caves of air,
And, daring the starlight above the stiff sea of cloud,
Deadly as a falcon brooding over its prey
In a tower of spirit-dazzling and splendid light,
Pedestrian man holds grimly on his way.
Legions of winds, ambushed in crystal corries,
Conspiring to destroy him, and hosts of ice,
Thronging him close, weigh down his delicate wings;
But loud as a drum in his ear the hot blood sings,
And a frenzy of solitude mantles him like a god.

DEATH OF A PEASANT

You remember Davies? He died, you know,
With his face to the wall, as the manner is
Of the poor peasant in his stone croft
On the Welsh hills. I recall the room
Under the slates, and the smirched snow
Of the wide bed in which he lay,
Lonely as an ewe that is sick to lamb
In the hard weather of mid-March.
I remember also the trapped wind
Tearing the curtains, and the wild light's
Frequent hysteria upon the floor,
The bare floor without a rug
Or mat to soften the loud tread
Of neighbours crossing the uneasy boards
To peer at Davies with gruff words
Of meaningless comfort, before they turned
Heartless away from the stale smell
Of death in league with those dank walls.

WELSH LANDSCAPE

To live in Wales is to be conscious
At dusk of the spilled blood
That went to the making of the wild sky,
Dyeing the immaculate rivers
In all their courses.
It is to be aware,
Above the noisy tractor
And hum of the machine
Of strife in the strung woods,
Vibrant with sped arrows.
You cannot live in the present,
At least not in Wales.
There is the language for instance,
The soft consonants
Strange to the ear.
There are cries in the dark at night
As owls answer the moon,
And thick ambush of shadows,
Hushed at the fields' corners.
There is no present in Wales,
And no future;
There is only the past,
Brittle with relics,
Wind-bitten towers and castles
With sham ghosts;
Mouldering quarries and mines;
And an impotent people,
Sick with inbreeding,
Worrying the carcase of an old song.

SOIL

A field with tall hedges and a young
Moon in the branches and one star
Declining westward set the scene
Where he works slowly astride the rows
Of red mangolds and green swedes
Plying mechanically his cold blade.

This is his world, the hedge defines
The mind's limits; only the sky
Is boundless, and he never looks up;
His gaze is deep in the dark soil,
As are his feet. The soil is all;
His hands fondle it, and his bones
Are formed out of it with the swedes.
And if sometimes the knife errs,
Burying itself in his shocked flesh,
Then out of the wound the blood seeps home
To the warm soil from which it came.

THE VILLAGE

Scarcely a street, too few houses
To merit the title; just a way between
The one tavern and the one shop
That leads nowhere and fails at the top
Of the short hill, eaten away
By long erosion of the green tide
Of grass creeping perpetually nearer
This last outpost of time past.

So little happens; the black dog
Cracking his fleas in the hot sun
Is history. Yet the girl who crosses
From door to door moves to a scale
Beyond the bland day's two dimensions.

Stay, then, village, for round you spins
On slow axis a world as vast
And meaningful as any poised
By great Plato's solitary mind.

AUTUMN ON THE LAND

A man, a field, silence—what is there to say?
He lives, he moves, and the October day
Burns slowly down.
                    History is made
Elsewhere; the hours forfeit to time's blade
Don't matter here. The leaves large and small,
Shed by the branches, unlamented fall

About his shoulders. You may look in vain
Through the eyes' window; on his meagre hearth
The thin, shy soul has not begun its reign
Over the darkness. Beauty, love and mirth
And joy are strangers there.
                              You must revise
Your bland philosophy of nature, earth
Has of itself no power to make men wise.

A BLACKBIRD SINGING

It seems wrong that out of this bird,
Black, bold, a suggestion of dark
Places about it, there yet should come
Such rich music, as though the notes'
Ore were changed to a rare metal
At one touch of that bright bill.

You have heard it often, alone at your desk
In a green April, your mind drawn
Away from its work by sweet disturbance
Of the mild evening outside your room.

A slow singer, but loading each phrase
With history's overtones, love, joy
And grief learned by his dark tribe
In other orchards and passed on
Instinctively as they are now,
But fresh always with new tears.

REASON FOR NOT WRITING ORTHODOX
NATURE POETRY

The January sky is deep and calm.   *John*
The mountain sprawls in comfort, and the sea   *Wain*
Sleeps in the crook of that enormous arm.

And Nature from a simple recipe—
Rocks, water, mist, a sunlit winter's day—
Has brewed a cup whose strength has dizzied me.

So little beauty is enough to pay;
The heart so soon yields up its store of love,
And where you love you cannot break away.

So sages never found it hard to prove
Nor prophets to declare in metaphor
That God and Nature must be hand in glove.

And this became the basis of their lore.
Then later poets found it easy going
To give the public what they bargained for,

And like a spectacled curator showing
The wares of his museum to the crowd,
They yearly waxed more eloquent and knowing

More slick, more photographic, and more proud:
From Tennyson with notebook in his hand
(His truth to Nature fits him like a shroud)

To moderns who devoutly hymn the land.
So be it: each is welcome to his voice;
They are a gentle, if a useless, band.

But leave me free to make a sterner choice;
Content, without embellishment, to note
How little beauty bids the heart rejoice,

How little beauty catches at the throat,
Simply, I love this mountain and this bay
With love that I can never speak by rote,

And where you love you cannot break away.

LAPWING

Rex
Warner

Leaves, summer's coinage spent, golden are all together whirled,
sent spinning, dipping, slipping, shuffled by heavy handed wind,
shifted sideways, sifted, lifted, and in swarms made to fly,
spent sunflies, gorgeous tatters, airdrift, pinions of trees.

Pennons of the autumn wind, flying the same loose flag,
minions of the rush of air, companions of draggled cloud,
tattered, scattered pell mell, diving, with side-slip suddenly wailing
as they scale the uneasy sky flapping the lapwing fly.

Plover, with under the tail pine-red, dead leafwealth in down
    displayed,
crested with glancing crests, sheeny with seagreen, mirror of movement
of the deep sea horses plunging, restless, fretted by the whip of wind
tugging green tons, wet waste, lugging a mass to Labrador.

See them fall wailing over high hill tops with hue and cry,
like uneasy ghosts slipping in the dishevelled air,
with ever so much of forlorn ocean and wastes of wind
in their elbowing of the air and in their lamentable call.

LONGTAILED TIT

All the spinney is active with churr and bat-squeak,
with flutter, flit, dip, dropping buoyant of bodies through the air,
jostling of cones, twig springing, twirling to ground of needles,
as tits and goldcrests swing and hustle in the bunchy trees.

Busy the goldcrest, high squeaking, under the needly
green fall of leaf forgetting the North Sea,
in inches of light whole-hearted, a spot of spirit.

The longtail lunging and lingering through the air,
a mouse, rush-tail, a ball, wool-feather, peeper,
looking so sharp through cherry blankets of down,
the doll-face easy on the flying twig's trapeze,
pink and white in the light, as light as blowing seed,
is meek in merriment, all careless of air's bitterness,
the bare-tooth coming, bark-biting of the winter wind.

THE COLLIER

When I was born on Amman hill   *Vernon*
A dark bird crossed the sun.   *Watkins*
Sharp on the floor the shadow fell;
I was the youngest son.

And when I went to the County School
I worked in a shaft of light.
In the wood of the desk I cut my name:
Dai for Dynamite.

169

The tall black hills my brothers stood;
Their lessons all were done.
From the door of the school when I ran out
They frowned to watch me run.

The slow grey bells they rung a chime
Surly with grief or age.
Clever or clumsy, lad or lout,
All would look for a wage.

I learnt the valley flowers' names
And the rough bark knew my knees,
I brought home trout from the river
And spotted eggs from the trees.

A coloured coat I was given to wear
Where the lights of the rough land shone.
Still jealous of my favour
The tall black hills looked on.

They dipped my coat in the blood of a kid
And they cast me down a pit,
And although I crossed with strangers
There was no way up from it.

Soon as I went from the County School
I worked in a shaft. Said Jim,
'You will get your chain of gold, my lad,
But not for a likely time.'

And one said, 'Jack was not raised up
When the wind blew out the light
Though he interpreted their dreams
And guessed their fears by night.'

And Tom, he shivered his leper's lamp
For the stain that round him grew;
And I heard mouths pray in the after-damp
When the picks would not break through.

They changed words there in darkness
And still through my head they run,
And white on my limbs is the linen sheet
And gold on my neck the sun.

AUTUMN SONG

Sycamores must fade,
Yellow acorns be lost,
Before this ghost be laid
In earth, in frost.

Then will this Jack of green
With mouth of leaves, this mummer
Be no more seen,
Sunk with the Summer,

Though now the stops he shuts
With minstrelsy
Slant eyes of buried nuts
Can hardly see,

Then shall his hands be taught.
Hush, he'll forget
How the blue sloes were caught
In grasses wet.

And here, where meet
The lines of heart and head,
Where softest words are sweet,
Words for the dead,

His cap of light, his bells
Shall faded play
Among the broken shells
In disarray.

THE JUNIPER TREE

Meet me my love, meet me my love   *Wilfred*
By the low branching juniper tree   *Watson*
O I will meet you there my love
If no harm come to me
If no harm come to me

Blue burns the cone, blue burns the cone
Of the low branching juniper tree
And there he waited for his love
As the black minutes go by
As the black minutes go by

Bellows in the field a cow, in the field a cow
Bellows loud after its dead calf
As he waited by the juniper tree
And he heard the red fox cough
He heard the red fox cough

Flew through the air, flew through the air an owl
To the low branching juniper tree
As he waited there for his love
And the black minutes went by
And the black minutes went by

The wind blew down, the wind blew down
Into the low branching juniper tree
And all the seeds rattled in the weed
As the wind blew sudden by
As the wind blew sudden by

Then fell the rain, then fell the rain down
Fell cold into black wet sleet
On the low branching juniper tree
And he said why is she late
He said why is she late

I have come to you my love, my love
Waiting by the juniper tree
And he turns to see her standing there
As white as death was she
As white as death was she

Then why are you so long my love, my love
As I waited at the juniper tree?
But now I will kiss your mouth, he said
O never you will, said she
O never you will, said she

THE MOMENT
The Trout Inn, near Tiverton

Margaret
Willy

From the white dance and dazzle of the river
Flashing through banks buttered with daffodils,
Out of the silver wind and flying sunlight
That mellows now across the rose-red hills

Come in to taste the warmth: the small flames' rustle,
The curled, contented cat, and humming room
Smoky of beam, ripe as an autumn pippin,
The sun-glint playing through the chestnut gloom;

Threading the haze, the burr and blur of voices,
Striking out fire from rows of burnished brass;
Ruddy it gilds the firkins and the faces,
And amber-brims the raised and chinking glass.

All—with that window-square of green-and-whiteness
Where jonquils toss, and cherry snows the grass—
Fuse in one glow: sun-shot and wind-lit blossom,
Fire, face and voice, weaving the living moment,
Charged with the loveliness of things that pass.

AN OLD LABOURER

Here was no shivering winter, nipped and sere,
Its music muted and the sap run dry;
But the full harvest of a mellowing year
Serene beneath the late October sky.
Laden, these boughs, with fruit of toiling days:
His pipe and ale; farm-gossip with a friend;
A lover's wonder in the fields' quiet ways
Burning still clearer here at autumn's end.

Undimmed these eyes that watched the seasons change
From cowslip days to mist and woods aflame,
Till seventy years rolled back towards his birth;
The harvest ripe, he feared in death no strange
Dark enemy—but calm when twilight came,
Lay down to join his old, first love, the earth.

A FUNERAL ORATION

Composed at thirty, my funeral oration: Here lies
David John Murray Wright, 6′ 2″, myopic blue eyes;
Hair grey (very distinguished looking, so I am told);
Shabbily dressed as a rule; susceptible to cold;

David
Wright

Acquainted with what are known as the normal vices;
Perpetually short of cash; useless in a crisis;
Preferring cats, hated dogs; drank (when he could) too much;
Was deaf as a tombstone; and extremely hard to touch.
Academic achievements: B.A., Oxon (2nd class);
Poetic: the publication of one volume of verse,
Which in his thirtieth year attained him no fame at all
Except among intractable poets, and a small
Lunatic fringe congregating in Soho pubs.
He could roll himself cigarettes from discarded stubs,
Assume the first position of Yoga; sail, row, swim;
And though deaf, in church appear to be joining a hymn.
Often arrested for being without a permit,
Starved on his talents as much as he dined on his wit,
Born in a dominion to which he hoped not to go back
Since predisposed to imagine white possibly black:
His life, like his times, was appalling; his conduct odd;
He hoped to write one good line; died believing in God.

COOLE PARK, 1929

W. B. Yeats

I meditate upon a swallow's flight,
Upon an aged woman and her house,
A sycamore and lime-tree lost in night
Although that western cloud is luminous,
Great works constructed there in nature's spite
For scholars and for poets after us,
Thoughts long knitted into a single thought,
A dance-like glory that those walls begot.

There Hyde before he had beaten into prose
That noble blade the Muses buckled on,
There one that ruffled in a manly pose
For all his timid heart, there that slow man,
That meditative man, John Synge, and those
Impetuous men, Shawe-Taylor and Hugh Lane,
Found pride established in humility,
A scene well set and excellent company.

They came like swallows and like swallows went,
And yet a woman's powerful character
Could keep a swallow to its first intent;
And half a dozen in formation there,

That seemed to whirl upon a compass-point,
Found certainty upon the dreaming air,
The intellectual sweetness of those lines
That cut through time or cross it withershins.

Here, traveller, scholar, poet, take your stand
When all those rooms and passages are gone,
When nettles wave upon a shapeless mound
And saplings root among the broken stone,
And dedicate—eyes bent upon the ground,
Back turned upon the brightness of the sun
And all the sensuality of the shade—
A moment's memory to that laurelled head.

COOLE PARK AND BALLYLEE, 1931

Under my window-ledge the waters race,
Otters below and moor-hens on the top,
Run for a mile undimmed in Heaven's face
Then darkening through 'dark' Raftery's 'cellar' drop,
Run underground, rise in a rocky place
In Coole demesne, and there to finish up
Spread to a lake and drop into a hole.
What's water but the generated soul?

Upon the border of that lake's a wood
Now all dry sticks under a wintry sun,
And in a copse of beeches there I stood,
For Nature's pulled her tragic buskin on
And all the rant's a mirror of my mood:
At sudden thunder of the mounting swan
I turned about and looked where branches break
The glittering reaches of the flooded lake.

Another emblem there! That stormy white
But seems a concentration of the sky;
And, like the soul, it sails into the sight
And in the morning's gone, no man knows why;
And is so lovely that it sets to right
What knowledge or its lack had set awry,
So arrogantly pure, a child might think
It can be murdered with a spot of ink.

Sound of a stick upon the floor, a sound
From somebody that toils from chair to chair;
Beloved books that famous hands have bound,
Old marble heads, old pictures everywhere;
Great rooms where travelled men and children found
Content or joy; a last inheritor
Where none has reigned that lacked a name and fame
Or out of folly into folly came.

A spot whereon the founders lived and died
Seemed once more dear than life; ancestral trees,
Or gardens rich in memory glorified
Marriages, alliances and families,
And every bride's ambition satisfied.
Where fashion or mere fantasy decrees
We shift about—all that great glory spent—
Like some poor Arab tribesman and his tent.

We were the last romantics—chose for theme
Traditional sanctity and loveliness;
Whatever's written in what poets name
The book of the people; whatever most can bless
The mind of man or elevate a rhyme;
But all is changed, that high horse riderless,
Though mounted in that saddle Homer rode
Where the swan drifts upon a darkening flood.

HARD FROST

*Andrew
Young*

Frost called to water 'Halt!'
And crusted the moist snow with sparkling salt;
Brooks, their own bridges, stop,
And icicles in long stalactites drop,
And tench in water-holes
Lurk under gluey glass like fish in bowls.

In the hard-rutted lane
At every footstep breaks a brittle pane,
And tinkling trees ice-bound,
Changed into weeping willows, sweep the ground;
Dead boughs take root in ponds
And ferns on windows shoot their ghostly fronds.

But vainly the fierce frost
Interns poor fish, ranks trees in an armed host,
Hangs daggers from house-eaves
And on the windows ferny ambush weaves;
In the long war grown warmer
The sun will strike him dead and strip his armour.

SNOW

Ridged thickly on black bough
   And foaming on twig-fork in swollen lumps
At flirt of bird-wing or wind's sough
   Plump snow tumbled on snow softly with sudden dumps.

Where early steps had made
   A wavering track through the white-blotted road
Breaking its brightness with blue shade
   Snow creaked beneath my feet with snow heavily shod.

I reached a snow-thatched rick
   Where men sawed bedding off for horse and cow;
There varnished straws were lying thick
   Paving with streaky gold the trodden silver snow.
Such light filled me with awe
   And nothing marred my paradisal thought,
That robin least of all I saw
   Lying too fast asleep, his song choked in his throat.

STAY, SPRING

Stay, spring, for by this ruthless haste
You turn all good to waste;
Look, how the blackthorn now
Changes to trifling dust upon the bough.

Where blossom from the wild pear shakes
Too rare a china breaks,
And though the cuckoos shout
They will forget their name ere June is out.

That thrush too, that with beadlike eye
Watches each passer-by,
Is warming at her breast
A brood that when they fly rob their own nest.

So late begun, so early ended!
Lest I should be offended
Take warning, spring, and stay
Or I might never turn to look your way.

THE SCARECROW

He strides across the grassy corn
That has not grown since it was born,
A piece of sacking on a pole,
A ghost, but nothing like a soul.

Why must this dead man haunt the spring
With arms anxiously beckoning?
Is spring not hard enough to bear
For one at autumn of his year?

THE ELM BEETLE

So long I sat and conned
That naked bole
With the strange hieroglyphics scored
That those small priests,
The beetle-grubs, had bored,
Telling of gods and kings and beasts
And the long journey of the soul
Through magic-opened gates
To where the throned Osiris waits,
That when at last I woke
I stepped from an Egyptian tomb
To see the wood's sun-spotted gloom,
And rising cottage smoke
That leaned upon the wind and broke,
Roller-striped fields, and smooth cow-shadowed pond.

THE BEECHWOOD

When the long, varnished buds of beech
Point out beyond their reach,
And tanned by summer suns
Leaves of black bryony turn bronze,
And gossamer floats bright and wet
From trees that are their own sunset,
Spring, summer, autumn I come here,
And what is there to fear?

And yet I never lose the feeling
That someone close behind is stealing
Or else in front has disappeared;
Though nothing I have seen or heard,
The fear of what I might have met
Makes me still walk beneath these boughs
With cautious step as in a haunted house.

THE ROUND BARROW

A lark as small as a flint arrow
Rises and falls over this ancient barrow
And seems to mock with its light tones
The silent man of bones;

Some prince that earth drew back again
From his long strife with wind and mist and rain,
Baring for him this broad round breast
In token of her rest.

But as I think how Death sat once
And with sly fingers picked those princely bones,
I feel my bones are verily
The stark and final I.

I climbed the hill housed in warm flesh,
But now as one escaped from its false mesh
Through the wan mist I journey on,
A clanking skeleton.

179

THE SWEDES

Andrew
Young

Three that are one since time began,
Horse, cart and man,
Lurch down the lane patched with loose stones;
Swedes in the cart heaped smooth and round
Like skulls that from the ground
The man has dug without the bones
Leave me in doubt
Whether the swedes with gold shoots sprout
Or with fresh fancies bursts each old bald sconce.

AUTUMN MIST

So thick a mist hung over all,
Rain had no room to fall;
It seemed a sea without a shore;
The cobwebs drooped heavy and hoar
As though with wool they had been knit;
Too obvious mark for fly to hit!

And though the sun was somewhere else
The gloom had brightness of its own
That shone on bracken, grass and stone
And mole-mound with its broken shells
That told where squirrel lately sat,
Cracked hazel-nuts and ate the fat.

And sullen haws in the hedgerows
Burned in the damp with clearer fire;
And brighter still than those
The scarlet hips hung on the briar
Like coffins of the dead dog-rose;
All were as bright as though for earth
Death were a gayer thing than birth.

FIELD-GLASSES

Though buds still speak in hints
And frozen ground has set the flints
As fast as precious stones
And birds perch on the boughs, silent as cones,

Suddenly waked from sloth
Young trees put on a ten years' growth
And stones double their size,
Drawn nearer through field-glasses' greater eyes.

Why I borrow their sight
Is not to give small birds a fright
Creeping up close by inches;
I make the trees come, bringing tits and finches.

I lift a field itself
As lightly as I might a shelf,
And the rooks do not rage
Caught for a moment in my crystal cage.

And while I stand and look,
Their private lives an open book,
I feel so privileged
My shoulders prick, as though they were half-fledged.

WILTSHIRE DOWNS

The cuckoo's double note
Loosened like bubbles from a drowning throat
Floats through the air
In mockery of pipit, lark and stare.

The stable-boys thud by
Their horses slinging divots at the sky
And with bright hooves
Printing the sodden turf with lucky grooves.

As still as a windhover
A shepherd in his flapping coat leans over
His tall sheep-crook
And shearlings, tegs and yoes cons like a book.
And one tree-crowned long barrow
Stretched like a sow that has brought forth her farrow
Hides a king's bones
Lying like broken sticks among the stones.

NOTES ON SOME COMMONWEALTH,
SOUTH AFRICAN AND AMERICAN AUTHORS

Conrad Aiken

Born in Georgia in 1889. Educated at Harvard. After the first World War he moved to Rye in Sussex, but now spends much of his time in America. He has been awarded the Pulitzer Prize, Bollingen Prize, a Guggenheim Fellowship and the Shelley Memorial Award. Besides many volumes of poems, he has written several novels and short stories.

Poems: *Selected Poems* (1929), *Preludes for Memnon* (1931), *Time in the Rock* (1936), *Skylight One* (1951).

James K. Baxter

Born in Dunedin, 1926. He led a varied life as farm labourer, postman, foundryman, proof-reader and school-teacher. He graduated at Victoria University, Wellington and is now working in the School Publications Branch of the Department of Education, Wellington.

Poems: *Beyond the Palisade* (1944), *Blow, Wind of Fruitfulness* (1948), *The Fallen House* (1953), *In Fires of No Return* (1958), *Howrah Bridge and Other Poems* (autumn 1961).

Charles Brasch

Born in Dunedin, 1909, read Modern History at Oxford and then became a teacher. Returned to New Zealand after the last war. Editor of *Landfall*, the New Zealand quarterly.

Poems: *Disputed Ground, Poems 1939–45* (1948), *The Estate and Other Poems* (1957).

Joseph Payne Brennan

Born in 1918. Works as an Assistant Librarian in New Haven, Connecticut. He edits two magazines, *Essence* and *Macabre*, and his own work has appeared in most of the best-known literary reviews in America.

Poems: *Heart of Earth, The Humming Stair*.

Jean Burden

A native of Illinois and a graduate of the University of Chicago. She now lives in Altadena, California. She is poetry editor and West Coast editor of the magazine *Yankee*. Besides her poetry, she is interested in, and writes on, Oriental religions.

David Campbell

Born at Ellerslie Station, near Adelong, New South Wales, 1915. A Cambridge graduate, he was a pilot in the Royal Australian Air Force during the war, and now owns a farm near Canberra.

Poems: *Speak with the Sun* (1949), *The Miracle of Mullion Hill* (1949).

Roy Campbell (1901–1957)

Born in South Africa, 1901. He joined the 6th South African Infantry at the age of fifteen and came to Europe in 1919. He fought in the Spanish

Civil War and volunteered for the British Army in 1939. He was per‐manently disabled during training and this ended his peace‐time occupa‐tions of horse‐breaker and bull‐fighter.

Poems: *Adamastor* (1928), *The Georgiad* (1931), *Flowering Reeds* (1933), *Talking Bronco* (1940).

E. E. Cummings (*1894–1962*)

Born in Cambridge, Massachusetts, he took his M.A. at Harvard in 1916 and went to France with an Ambulance Corps. He was Norton Professor of Poetry at Harvard from 1952 to 1953.

Poems: *Collected Poems* (1938), *50 Poems* (1940), *1 × 1* (1944), *Selected Poems* (1960).

James Devaney

Born in Bendigo, Victoria in 1890, and educated at St Joseph's College, Sydney. He works as a freelance journalist and literary critic.

Poems: *Where the Wind Goes* (1939), *Freight of Dreams* (1946), *Washdirt* (1947), *Selected Poems* (1950).

Basil Dowling

Born at Southridge, Canterbury, New Zealand in 1910, and educated at St Andrew's College and Canterbury University College. From 1947 to 1951 he was a librarian in New Zealand. Since 1952 he has been a schoolmaster in England.

Poems: *A Day's Journey* (1941), *Signs and Wonders* (1944), *Canterbury and Other Poems* (1949).

Eileen Duggan

Born in Tuamarina, New Zealand. She has been a schoolmistress, and a lecturer in history at Victoria College. She contributes verse and literary criticism to papers in New Zealand and abroad.

Poems: *New Zealand Poems* (1940), *More Poems* (1951).

Richard Eberhart

Born in 1904 in Austin, Minnesota. He was educated at Dartmouth and Harvard, and at St John's College, Cambridge. He has been Professor of English and Poet in Residence at Dartmouth since 1956. He was a founder and first president of the Poet's Theatre, Cambridge, Mass. in 1951. He has won several major awards for his poetry, including the Shelley Memorial Prize in 1951.

Poems: *Burr Oaks* (1947), *Selected Poems* (1951), *Undercliff* (1954), *Great Praises* (1957).

A. R. D. Fairburn (*1904–1957*)

Although a lecturer at the University of Auckland from 1951 to 1957, he had previously worked as clerk, journalist, radio script‐writer and Farmers' Union Secretary. A prolific writer of pamphlets on various subjects.

Poems: *Strange Rendezvous* (1952), *Three Poems* (1952).

Robert Frost (1875–1963)

Born in San Francisco and educated at Dartmouth and Harvard Colleges. After various occupations, including teaching and cobbling, he came to England in 1912. By the time he returned to America in 1916 he had made his name as a poet. He won the Pulitzer Prize for poetry in 1924, 1931, 1937 and 1943, and was Honorary President of the Poetry Society of America.

Poems: *North of Boston* (1914), *Mountain Interval* (1916), *New Hampshire* (1923), *Complete Poems* (1951).

Mary Fullerton (1868–1946)

Born in Glenmaggie, North Gippsland, Victoria in 1868. She came to England in 1921. As well as being a poet, she was a journalist and novelist.

Poems: *The Breaking Furrow* (1921), *Moles do so Little with their Privacy* (1942), *The Wonder and the Apple* (1946).

William Hart-Smith

Born at Tunbridge Wells, Kent, 1911. He emigrated to New Zealand in 1924 and became a radio mechanic at the age of fifteen. He lived in Australia from 1936 to 1947, when he returned to New Zealand.

Poems: *Christopher Columbus* (1948), *On the Level* (1950), *Poems of Discovery* (1959).

Rex Ingamells (1913–1955)

A graduate of Adelaide University, he was first a school-teacher and then an educational representative. The founder of the literary movement known as the Jindyworobak Club, which specially emphasized aboriginal culture.

Poems: *Selected Poems* (1944), *The Great South Land* (1951).

Randall Jarrell

Born at Nashville, Tennessee, in 1914. He served during the war in the U.S.A.A.F. He has taught in various colleges in the United States, and is now a Professor of English in the University of North Carolina. Besides poetry, he has written novels and short stories.

Poems: *Blood for a Stranger* (1942), *Little Friend, Little Friend* (1945), *Losses* (1948), *The Seven League Crutches* (1951).

Robinson Jeffers

Born in Pittsburgh, Pennsylvania, 1887. After studying in Switzerland and America he settled near Carmel, North California and has produced many books of verse.

Poems: *Selected Poems* (1937), *Such Counsels You Gave Me* (1937), *Be Angry at the Sun* (1941), *The Double Axe* (1948).

M. K. Joseph

Born in London, 1914. Emigrated in 1924 to New Zealand. Studied at the University of Auckland and Merton College, Oxford. Returned to University of Auckland in 1946 after war service. Now associate professor in English.

Poems: *Imaginary Islands* (1950), *The Living Countries* (1959).

Dorothy Livesay
Born in Winnipeg, 1909. After studying at the University of Toronto and the Sorbonne she became a teacher in Vancouver.

Poems: *Selected Poems* (1957).

R. A. K. Mason
Born in Auckland, New Zealand, 1905. After graduating from the University of Auckland he became a teacher, and has since followed various occupations, including landscape gardening.

Poems: *This Dark Will Lighten, Selected Poems 1923-41* (1941), *Recent Poems* (1943).

Edna St Vincent Millay (1892-1950)
Born in Maine and worked as a freelance in New York until her marriage in 1923.

Poems: *Collected Sonnets* (1941), *Collected Lyrics* (1943).

W. H. Oliver
Born at Feilding, Wellington, New Zealand. Educated at Victoria University of Wellington, 1925 and Oxford, and is now a lecturer in history at Victoria University.

Poems: *Fire without Phoenix, Poems 1946-54* (1957).

William Plomer
Born at Pietersburg, N. Transvaal, South Africa in 1903. Educated at Rugby. He has travelled widely, especially in Greece and Japan. As well as poetry, he writes novels, short stories and essays.

Poems: *Collected Poems* (1960).

E. J. Pratt
Born at Western Bay, Newfoundland in 1883. Taught English at the University of Toronto until his retirement in 1952. He is editor of the *Canadian Poetry Magazine*.

Poems: *Collected Poems* (1944), *They are Returning* (1945), *Behind the Log* (1947), *Towards the Last Spike* (1952).

John Crowe Ransom
Born in Pulaski, Tennessee, 1888. From Vanderbilt University he went to Oxford. In 1914 he returned to Vanderbilt as a member of the English faculty.

Poems: *Selected Poems* (1945).

Charles G. D. Roberts (1860-1943)
Educated at the University of New Brunswick and became a teacher. He travelled extensively in the United States and England.

Poems: *Selected Poems* (1955).

SOURCES AND ACKNOWLEDGMENTS

Thanks are due to the authors (or their executors), their representatives and publishers mentioned in the following list for their kind permission to reproduce copyright material:

Conrad Aiken (A. M. Heath and Co. Ltd): 'All lovely things' from *Collected Poems of Conrad Aiken* (Oxford University Press; copyright 1929, 1957, by Conrad Aiken).

John Arlott: 'Brighton', 'Tea with My Aunts' and 'A Little Guide to Winchester' from *Of Period and Place* (Jonathan Cape Ltd).

W. H. Auden: 'O what is that sound', 'Refugee Blues', 'Musée des Beaux Arts' and 'As I walked out one evening' from *Collected Shorter Poems 1930–44* (Faber and Faber Ltd).

James K. Baxter: 'Wild Bees' from *The Fallen House* (The Caxton Press).

Bernard Bergonzi: 'Anemones for Miss Austen' from *Descartes and The Animals* (Platform Press).

John Betjeman: 'On a Portrait of a Deaf Man', 'Death in Leamington', 'The Village Inn', 'Christmas', 'Bristol' and 'Sunday Morning, King's Cambridge' from *Collected Poems*, and 'Cornwall in Childhood' from *Summoned by Bells* (John Murray (Publishers) Ltd).

Laurence Binyon (The Society of Authors and Mrs Cicely Binyon): 'History' from *Collected Poems* and 'The Burning of the Leaves' from *The Burning of the Leaves* (Macmillan).

Edmund Blunden: 'The Midnight Skaters', 'The Giant Puff ball', 'Brook in Drought', 'Bells', 'Triumph of Autumn', 'Departed' and 'The Pike' from *Poems of Many Years* (William Collins Sons and Co. Ltd).

Charles Brasch: 'Poland, October' from *Disputed Ground, Poems 1939–45* (The Caxton Press).

Joseph Payne Brennan: 'Grey Owl' (*The University of Kansas City Review*, Stanford University Press).

Gerald Bullett: 'The Church Mouse' from *News from the Village* (Cambridge University Press).

Jean Burden: 'Final Stone' (published in *The Southwest Review*).

David Campbell: 'Men in Green' from *Speak with the Sun* (The Hogarth Press Ltd).

Roy Campbell (Curtis Brown Ltd); 'The Theology of Bongwi, the Baboon', 'The Serf', 'Autumn' and 'African Moonrise' from *Adamastor*. 'Washing Day' from *Talking Bronco* (Faber and Faber Ltd).

Richard Church: 'Archaeology', 'Small Mercies, 1934', 'Housing Scheme', 'The Warning' and 'Piccadilly Pastoral' from *The Collected Poems* (J. M. Dent and Sons Ltd).

Henry Compton: 'The Visitor', 'Steel' and 'Immortality' from *Kindred Points* (George Allen and Unwin Ltd).

Frances Cornford: 'Travelling Home' from *Collected Poems* (The Cresset Press).

E. E. Cummings: 'Anyone lived in a pretty how town', 'What if a much of a which of a wind', 'Spring is like a perhaps hand' and 'In Just-' from *Selected Poems* (Faber and Faber Ltd).

Paul Dehn: 'Lament for a Sailor' from *The Day's Alarm* (Hamish Hamilton Ltd).

Walter de la Mare (The Literary Trustees and The Society of Authors as their representative): 'Memory', 'Solitude', 'Tarbury Steep', 'The Last Guest' and 'Frescoes in an Old Church' from *Collected Poems* (Faber and Faber Ltd).

James Devaney: 'Mortality' from *Poems* (Angus and Robertson Ltd).

Basil Dowling: 'Naseby: Late Autumn' from *Arts in New Zealand* (published by Harry H. Tombs Ltd).

Eileen Duggan: 'Contrast' from *More Poems* (George Allen and Unwin Ltd).

Clifford Dyment: 'The Axe in the Wood' and 'The Winter Trees' from *The Axe in the Wood*, and 'The Wayfarer' from *Poems 1935–48* (J. M. Dent and Sons Ltd).

Richard Eberhart: 'Burden' from *Collected Poems* (The Hogarth Press Ltd).

T. S. Eliot: 'Journey of the Magi' and 'Chorus from "The Rock"' from *Collected Poems 1909–35*, and extract from 'The Dry Salvages' from *Four Quartets* (Faber and Faber Ltd).

D. J. Enright: 'The "Black" Country' from *The Laughing Hyena* (Routledge and Kegan Paul Ltd).

A. R. D. Fairburn: 'Night Song' from *Strange Rendezvous* (The Caxton Press Ltd); 'Song at Summer's End' from *Arts Year Book 1947* (Harry H. Tombs Ltd).

Robert Farren: 'All That Is, and Can Delight'.

Yvonne ffrench: 'Daybreak in the Tropics'.

Robert Frost: 'Unharvested', 'There are Roughly Zones' and 'Acceptance' from *The Complete Poems* (Jonathan Cape Ltd and Henry Holt and Co. Inc.).

Roy Fuller: 'The Snow', 'Time', 'The Image', 'Preface to an Anthology' and 'Owls' from *Counterparts* (André Deutsch Ltd).

Mary Fullerton: 'A Dream' and 'Passivity' from *Moles do so Little with their Privacy* (Angus and Robertson Ltd).

David Gascoyne: 'Spring MCMXL' and 'Snow in Europe' from *Poems 1937–42* (André Deutsch Ltd).

Stella Gibbons: 'The Giraffes', 'Coverings' and 'Lullaby for a Baby Toad' from *Collected Poems* (Longmans, Green and Co. Ltd).

Douglas Gibson: 'Another Spring' and 'At Broxbourne Station' from *The Singing Earth* (William Heinemann Ltd); 'The Stricken Tree' and 'Insensibility' from *Winter Journey and other Poems* (Jonathan Cape Ltd).

Wilfrid Gibson: 'The Blind-worm', 'The Last Shift' and 'The Feathers' from *Solway Ford* (Faber and Faber Ltd).

Robert Gittings: 'A Midwinter Scene' and 'Hibernation' from *Famous Meeting* (William Heinemann Ltd).

Robert Graves: 'The Haunted House', 'An English Wood', 'The Cool Web' and 'The Persian Version' from *Collected Poems 1959* (Cassell and Co. Ltd).

Geoffrey Grigson: 'New April' and 'Autumn Under the Trees' from *The Isles of Scilly* (Routledge and Kegan Paul Ltd).

Bryan Guinness: 'What Are They Thinking . . .' from *Reflexions* (William Heinemann Ltd).

J. C. Hall: 'The Wood' from *The Summer Dance* (John Lehmann).

Michael Hamburger: 'After Christmas' from *The Dual Site* (Routledge and Kegan Paul Ltd).

Sir George Rostrevor Hamilton: 'New Cities' and 'Hawk' from *Unknown Lovers and Other Poems* (William Heinemann Ltd).

W. Hart-Smith: 'Bathymeter' from *Bulletin*.

Phoebe Hesketh: 'The Fox' and 'Bleasdale: The Wooden Circle' from *The Buttercup Children* (Rupert Hart-Davis Ltd); 'The Invading Spring', 'In Autumn' and 'The Expert' from *Between Wheels and Stars* (William Heinemann Ltd).

Geoffrey Hill: 'Merlin' from *For The Unfallen* (André Deutsch Ltd).

Mark Holloway: 'The Quick and the Dead'.

Richard Hughes: 'Travel-piece' from *Confessio Juvenis* (The Hogarth Press Ltd).

Ted Hughes: 'The Horses' from *The Hawk in the Rain*, and 'Pike' from *Lupercal* (Faber and Faber Ltd).

Rex Ingamells: 'Sea-Chronicles' from *Australian Poetry* (Angus and Robertson Ltd).

Randall Jarrell: 'Prisoners' and 'The Metamorphoses' from *Collected Poems* (Faber and Faber Ltd).

Robinson Jeffers: 'The Purse-Seine' (copyright 1937 by Random House Inc.) reprinted by permission from *The Selected Poetry of Robinson Jeffers*; 'Their Beauty has more Meaning' reprinted by permission from *The Double Axe and Other Poems* (copyright by Random House Inc.).

Sean Jennett: 'Fighting in naked deserts he thought of home' from *Always Adam*, and 'I was a labourer in the smoky valley' from *The Cloth of Flesh* (Faber and Faber Ltd).

Geoffrey Johnson: 'Words', 'The Woodcarver', 'Undeceived' and 'In Hardware Street' from *The Iron Harvest* (Williams and Norgate Ltd).

M. K. Joseph: 'On the Mountain' from *The Living Countries* (Paul's Book Arcade); and 'Secular Litany' from *Imaginary Island*.

Sidney Keyes: 'William Wordsworth', 'Pheasant' and 'Against Divination' from *Collected Poems* (Routledge and Kegan Paul Ltd).

Carla Lanyon Lanyon: 'The White Moth' from *Unfamiliar Mountain* (Outposts Publications).

Philip Larkin: 'An Arundel Tomb'; also 'Born Yesterday' and 'Skin' from *The Less Deceived* (The Marvell Press, Hessle, Yorkshire).

D. H. Lawrence (the Estate of the late Mrs Frieda Lawrence): 'Bavarian Gentians', 'Bat' and 'Humming-Bird' from *The Complete Poems* (William Heinemann Ltd).

Christopher Lee: Extracts from 'April and Anglesey' from *Under The Sun* (The Bodley Head Ltd.)

Laurie Lee: 'Cock-pheasant' (reproduced by courtesy of *Vogue*); 'Field of Autumn' from *The Bloom of Candles* (John Lehmann Ltd); 'Sunken Evening' from *My Many-Coated Man* (André Deutsch Ltd).

John Lehmann: 'Waking from Snow' and 'A Blind Man' from *The Age of the Dragon* (Longmans, Green and Co. Ltd).

Alun Lewis: 'Indian Day' from *Ha! Ha! Among the Trumpets* (George Allen and Unwin Ltd).

C. Day Lewis: 'Jig', 'Hornpipe', 'Will It Be So Again?', 'When Nature Plays', 'But Two There Are . . .', 'Two Songs' and 'The Ecstatic' from *The Collected Poems* (Jonathan Cape Ltd).

Dorothy Livesay: 'Of Mourners' from *Poems for People* (The Ryerson Press, Toronto).

Norman MacCaig: 'Summer Farm' from *Riding Lights* (The Hogarth Press Ltd).

Donagh MacDonagh: 'A Warning to Conquerors': also 'Juvenile Delinquency' from *The Hungry Grass* (Faber and Faber Ltd).

Louis MacNeice: 'Prayer before Birth', 'Morning Sun' and 'Sunday Morning' from *Collected Poems 1925–48*, and 'Visit to Rouen' and 'Jigsaws II and III' from *Visitations* (Faber and Faber Ltd).

Dr John Masefield, O.M. (The Society of Authors): 'Posted' from *Collected Poems* by John Masefield. Copyright 1930 by the author. Used with the permission of The Macmillan Company.

R. A. K. Mason: 'After Death' from *This Dark will Lighten* (The Caxton Press).

Huw Menai: 'Hoar-Frost' from *The Simple Vision* (Chapman and Hall Ltd).

Edna St Vincent Millay: 'Tranquillity at length, when autumn comes', 'And if I die' and 'Read history' from *Mine the Harvest* (Hamish Hamilton), copyright 1941, 1949 and 1954 by Edna St Vincent Millay, Norma Millay Ellis and Curtis Publishing Co.

A. A. Milne: extract from *The Norman Church* (Methuen and Co. Ltd).

Edwin Muir: 'Scotland's Winter', 'Horses' and 'Suburban Dream' from *Collected Poems* (Faber and Faber Ltd).

Norman Nicholson: 'South Cumberland, 10 May 1943', 'Michaelmas', 'Shortest Day, 1942', 'Cleator Moor' and 'The Blackberry' from *Five Rivers*, and 'St Luke's Summer' from *Rock Face* (Faber and Faber Ltd).

W. H. Oliver: 'The Beachcomber' (published in the *New Zealand Listener*).

Ruth Pitter: 'Call not to me', 'The Lost Hermitage', 'The Bat', 'The Viper' and 'The Paradox' from *Urania* (The Cresset Press).

William Plomer: 'Namaqualand After Rain', 'A Levantine' and 'The Caledonian Market' from *Selected Poems* (The Hogarth Press Ltd).

E. J. Pratt: 'The Prize Cat' from *Collected Poems* (Macmillan and Co. Ltd).

John Pudney: 'July' from *Collected Poems* (Putnam and Co. Ltd).

John Crowe Ransom: 'Piazza Piece' from *Selected Poems* (Alfred A. Knopf Inc., New York).

Herbert Read: 'Epitaph' from *A World within a War* (Faber and Faber Ltd).

Henry Reed: 'Lessons of the War. 1: Naming of Parts' from *A Map of Verona* (Jonathan Cape Ltd).

James Reeves: 'Had I passion to match my skill', 'Leaving Town' and 'This is your elegy' from *The Password and Other Poems* (William Heinemann Ltd).

Sir Charles G. D. Roberts: 'The Flight of the Geese' from *The Collected Poems* (The Ryerson Press, Toronto).

W. R. Rodgers: 'The Harvest Field' and 'The Journey of the Magi' from *Europa and the Bull* (Martin Secker and Warburg).

Alan Ross: 'Night Patrol', 'Survivors', 'Autumn in Hyde Park', 'Zoo' and 'Basra: Experiment with Oil' from *Something of the Sea*, Published by Verschoyle Ltd (André Deutsch Ltd).

A. L. Rowse: 'Spring in Grove Alley' from *Poems of Deliverance* (Faber and Faber Ltd).

V. Sackville-West: three extracts from *The Land* (William Heinemann Ltd): two extracts from *The Garden* (Michael Joseph Ltd).

Siegfried Sassoon: 'Prehistoric Burials', 'Antiquities', 'Gloria Mundi' and 'Early Chronology'.

Vernon Scannell: 'Sonnet' from *Graves and Resurrections* (Fortune Press); and 'Schoolroom on a Wet Afternoon'.

Francis Scarfe: 'Canterbury in Winter' from *Underworlds* (William Heinemann Ltd).

Howard Sergeant: 'The Inarticulate' from *The Headlands* (Putnam and Co. Ltd); 'Intervention' from *The Leavening Air* (Fortune Press).

Stevie Smith: 'Not Waving but Drowning' from *Not Waving but Drowning* (André Deutsch Ltd).

Stanley Snaith: 'To Some Builders of Cities'; also 'Pylons' from *Green Legacy* (Jonathan Cape Ltd).

Bernard Spencer: 'Base Town' and 'Olive Trees'.

Stephen Spender: 'The Barn', 'I hear the cries of evening', 'An Elementary School Class Room in a Slum' and 'The Pylons' from *Collected Poems* (Faber and Faber Ltd).

Margaret Stanley-Wrench: 'The Submerged Cathedral, Selsey' (published in *Poetry Review*).

Dylan Thomas: 'Fern Hill', 'Do Not Go Gentle into That Good Night', 'And Death Shall Have No Dominion' and 'Especially when the October Wind' from *Collected Poems 1934-52* (J. M. Dent and Sons Ltd).

R. S. Thomas: 'Homo Sapiens 1941', 'Death of a Peasant', 'Welsh Landscape', 'Soil', 'The Village' and 'Autumn on the Land', from *Songs at the Year's Turning*, and 'A Blackbird Singing' from *Poetry for Supper* (Rupert Hart-Davis Ltd).

John Wain: 'Reason for Not Writing Orthodox Nature Poetry' from *A Word Carved on a Sill* (Routledge and Kegan Paul Ltd).

Rex Warner: 'Longtailed Tit' and 'Lapwing' from *Poems* (The Bodley Head Ltd).

Vernon Watkins: 'The Collier' and 'Autumn Song' from *Ballad of the Mari Lwyd* (Faber and Faber Ltd).

Wilfred Watson: 'The Juniper Tree' from *Friday's Child* (Faber and Faber Ltd).

Margaret Willy: 'The Moment' and 'An Old Labourer' from *Every Star a Tongue* (William Heinemann Ltd).

David Wright: 'A Funeral Oration' from *Moral Stories* (André Deutsch Ltd).

W. B. Yeats: 'Coole Park, 1929' and 'Coole Park and Ballylee, 1931' from *Collected Poems of W. B. Yeats* (Mrs W. B. Yeats and Macmillan & Co. Ltd).

Andrew Young: 'Wiltshire Downs', 'Hard Frost', 'Snow', 'The Scarecrow', 'The Elm Beetle', 'The Beechwood', 'The Round Barrow', 'The Swedes', 'Autumn Mist', 'Field-Glasses' and 'Stay, Spring' from *Collected Poems* (Rupert Hart-Davis Ltd).

INDEX OF FIRST LINES

191